DOS argentinos, campeones, rivales y amigos: FANGIO y GÁLVEZ.

LIVING IN ARGENTINA

PHOTOS RICARDO LABOUGLE
TEXT & PRODUCTION ANA CARDINALE / ISABEL DE ESTRADA

LIVING IN ARGENTINA

EDITED BY / HERAUSGEGEBEN VON / SOUS LA DIRECTION DE

ANGELIKA TASCHEN

TASCHEN

HONG KONG KÖLN LONDON LOS ANGELES MADRID PARIS TOKYO

Contents / Inhalt / Sommaire

TEATRO COLÓN

CENTRO, BUENOS AIRES

After a tragic start, the Colón Theatre was eventually inaugurated in 1908 with a production of the opera *Aida*. Francesco Tamburini and Vittorio Meano, the first two architects contracted to build the theatre, died shortly after work had begun. The Belgian architect Jules Dormal was then chosen to take over this prestigious task but was hesitant because of the fate that had befallen his predecessors. The theatre, with a seating capacity of 3,000, a horseshoe-shaped auditorium and a very large stage, became eclectic in style. "It will have elements of the Italian Renaissance combined with the layout and solidity of detail of German architecture, and the grace, variety and extravagance of French architecture," explained Vittorio Meano. The quality and acoustics of the Colón Theatre were among the best in the world and made it a sought after venue for many world famous performers. Celebrities such as Rudolf Nureyev, Maya Plissestkaya, Margot Fonteyn and Maria Callas crossed the Atlantic to appear on its stage. Renovation since 2006 has restored it to its former splendour.

9

Nach einem tragischen Baubeginn wurde das Teatro Colón 1908 mit der Oper *Aida* eröffnet. Die beiden ersten für den Bau verpflichteten Architekten, Francesco Tamburini und Vittorio Meano, starben kurz nach Beginn der Bauarbeiten, danach fiel die Wahl auf den belgischen Architekten Jules Dormal. Aufgrund des Todes seiner Vorgänger soll er lange gezögert haben, den bedeutenden Auftrag anzunehmen. Das Theater geriet zu einem eklektischen Bauwerk, mit Sitz- und Stehplätzen für knapp 3.000 Personen, einem hufeisenförmigen Grundriss und einer riesigen Bühne. „Es sollte die Merkmale der italienischen Renaissance aufweisen, verbunden mit der für die deutsche Architektur typischen Ordnung und Solidität sowie der Anmut, Vielfalt und Bizarrerie der französischen Architektur", sagte Vittorio Meano. Seiner Beschaffenheit und Akustik zufolge gehörte das Teatro Colón zu den besten Opernhäusern der Welt. Rudolf Nurejew, Maja Plissetzkaja, Margot Fonteyn oder Maria Callas überquerten den Ozean, um sich hier zu präsentieren. Das Theater erfährt seit dem Jahr 2006 eine umfassende Sanierung, um im alten Glanz wiederaufzuerstehen.

Le Colón fut inauguré en 1908 avec l'opéra *Aida* après des débuts tragiques. Ses deux premiers architectes, Francesco Tamburini et Vittorio Meano, moururent peu après le commencement des travaux. Le belge Jules Dormal prit leur relève, non sans avoir longuement hésité compte tenu du sort de ses prédécesseurs. Avec ses 3.000 places, son plan en fer à cheval et sa vaste scène, le théâtre est un édifice éclectique. Meano avait promis : « Il aura les caractéristiques de la Renaissance italienne, unissant la distribution et la rigueur des détails de l'architecture allemande à la grâce, la variété et la bizarrerie de la française. » Grâce à sa qualité et son acoustique, la salle est devenue l'une des meilleures du monde, attirant les plus grands artistes internationaux. Rudolf Noureïev, Maya Plissetskaïa, Margot Fonteyn ou Maria Callas, entre autres, s'y sont représentés. Aujourd'hui encore, opéra le plus dynamique d'Amérique du Sud, sa magie reste intacte. Depuis 2006, ce théâtre magnifique subit d'importants travaux de restauration afin de retrouver sa splendeur passée.

LEFT PAGE:
The theatre's original fire extinguisher mounted on one of the walls of the main foyer.

RIGHT PAGE:
Main entrance and foyer in Verona marble, leading to the Carrara marble staircase. The side passages off the main staircase lead to the "Pasaje de los Carruajes," a small interior street.

FOLLOWING DOUBLE PAGE:
The horseshoe-shaped auditorium with 2,478 seats is surrounded by boxes with carved fronts decorated in gold leaf.

LINKE SEITE:
Originaler Feuerwehrschlauch des Theaters, an einer Wand der Eingangshalle befestigt.

RECHTE SEITE:
Die Eingangstür und das mit Marmor ausgekleidete Vestibül, das zur Treppe aus Carrara-Marmor führt. Seitlich der Haupttreppe gelangt man in die Pasaje de los Carruajes, eine Passage im Inneren.

FOLGENDE DOPPELSEITE:
Der hufeisenförmige Zuschauerraum mit 2.478 Sitzplätzen wird von Logen umringt, deren Brüstungen mit vergoldeten Schnitzereien verziert sind.

PAGE DE GAUCHE :
Un extincteur d'origine, sur un mur du hall d'entrée.

PAGE DE DROITE :
La porte d'entrée et le vestibule en marbre de Vérone qui mène au grand escalier en marbre de Carrare. De chaque côté de l'entrée principale, on peut accéder au « passage des calèches ».

DOUBLE PAGE SUIVANTE :
La salle en fer à cheval, comptant 2.478 places, entourée de loges dont les façades sont dorées à la feuille.

10

The first-floor boxes are separated by velvet-covered curved partitions; the curtains are silk and cotton and the pelmets are embroidered in silver thread.

Die Logen in der unteren Etage sind durch geschwungene, mit Samt bezogene Trennwände unterteilt. Ihre Vorhänge bestehen aus Seide und Baumwolle, und ihre Bordüren sind mit Silberfäden durchwirkt.

Les loges du premier balcon, qui conservent leurs soieries d'origine, sont séparées par des cloisons tapissées de velours. Les rideaux sont en soie et coton. Les embrasses sont brodées de fils d'argent.

14

LEFT PAGE:
The central chandelier is seven metres in diameter, holds 700 light bulbs and is made of burnished bronze. The auditorium ceiling was restored in 1966 by the Argentinian painter Raúl Soldi who recreated the frescoes.

RIGHT PAGE:
The golden hall on the top floor covers 440 square metres and has carved columns with details in gold leaf, tall Versailles-style mirrors and large French chandeliers.

LINKE SEITE:
Kronleuchter aus polierter Bronze mit 700 Glühbirnen und einem Durchmesser von sieben Metern. Die Decke des Saals wurde 1966 von dem argentinischen Maler Raúl Soldi renoviert, der auch für die Fresken verantwortlich zeichnet.

RECHTE SEITE:
Der goldene Salon im oberen Geschoss mit einer Fläche von 440 Quadratmeter enthält geschnitzte Säulenkapitelle mit vergoldeten Details, hohe Spiegel à la Versailles und große Kronleuchter aus Frankreich.

16

PAGE DE GAUCHE :
Le lustre central, en bronze patiné, mesure sept mètres de diamètre et comporte 700 ampoules électriques. Le plafond de la salle fut rénové en 1966 par le peintre argentin Raúl Soldi qui l'a orné de fresques.

PAGE DE DROITE :
Le salon doré du dernier étage fait 440 mètre carré. Colonnes ornées de dorures, hauts miroirs à la Versailles et grands lustres français.

Casa Kálnay

RODOLFO MACHADO & JORGE SILVETTI
RETIRO, BUENOS AIRES

It was this 1936 apartment that decided Rodolfo Machado and Jorge Silvetti – two architects with prestigious academic and professional careers in the United States behind them – to put down roots again in their native city. The building, designed by Hungarian-born architect Jorge Kálnay, also responsible for other important buildings in the city, displays all the fine qualities that characterise this period in terms of its materials and finish. The building's entrance hall in Uruguay marble is a fine example of the city's 1930s modern architecture. Inside the apartment, the architects have left the layout of the rooms unaltered, restoring only the oak doors that had been covered in layers of paint, polishing up the geometric fittings and restoring the damaged oak flooring. As keen travellers with a passion for 20th-century Argentinian art, Machado and Silvetti have gradually furnished these spaces with interesting pieces they have picked up on their travels. Sculptures, lamps, armchairs and tables ranging from the 1920s to the 1970s provide the perfect accompaniment to Kálnay's austerely designed spaces.

LEFT PAGE:

Balcony with 1930 table designed by Gilbert Poillerat and 1930s English teapot and coffee pot. In the background is the Estrugamou Building, an example of early 20th-century French architecture.

RIGHT:

View of the 1936 building constructed by European born Argentinian architect Jorge Kálnay – a fine example of Argentinian Rationalist architecture in the Retiro district close to the railway station.

LINKE SEITE:

Englische Tee- und Kaffeekanne aus den 1930er-Jahren auf dem Balkontisch von Gilbert Poillerat. Im Hintergrund sieht man das Estrugamou-Gebäude vom Anfang des 20. Jahrhunderts.

RECHTS:

Blick auf das 1936 von Jorge Kálnay – einem argentinischen Architekten ungarischer Herkunft – errichtete Gebäude, ein Beispiel des argentinischen Rationalismus im Retiro-Viertel.

PAGE DE GAUCHE :

Sur le balcon, sur une table de Gilbert Poillerat de 1930, une théière et une cafetière anglaises des années 1930. En face, on aperçoit l'immeuble Estrugamou, caractéristique de l'influence française au début du 20ᵉ siècle.

À DROITE :

L'immeuble construit, en 1936 par Jorge Kálnay, est typique du style rationaliste argentin. Il se trouve dans le quartier du Retiro, près de la gare.

Ein Apartment aus dem Jahr 1936 bewog die Architekten Rodolfo Machado und Jorge Silvetti – die beide auf eine akademische und berufliche Karriere in den Vereinigten Staaten zurückblicken, wieder in ihre Heimatstadt zu ziehen. Das betreffende Gebäude des Architekten Jorge Kálnay, Schöpfer einiger bedeutender Bau-Ikonen in Buenos Aires, zeigt in Material und Ausführung die ganze Eleganz dieser Epoche. Die Eingangshalle des Gebäudes aus uruguayischem Marmor ist ein Beispiel für die moderne Architektur der 1930er-Jahre in Buenos Aires. Im Inneren der Wohnung ließen die beiden Architekten den Grundriss unverändert und restaurierten lediglich die mit Farbschichten bedeckten Türen aus Eichenholz, polierten die geometrischen Metallelemente und restaurierten das Eichenholzparkett. Die beiden Architekten, die gern reisen und sich für die argentinische Kunst des 20. Jahrhunderts begeistern, haben die Räume mit interessanten Mitbringseln ausgestattet. Skulpturen, Lampen, Sessel oder Tische aus der Zeit zwischen 1920 und 1970 beleben die von Kálnay konzipierten strengen Räume.

Rodolfo Machado et Jorge Silvetti, qui ont fait tous deux une brillante carrière aux États-Unis dans la construction et l'enseignement supérieur, ont décidé d'acheter un pied à terre dans leur ville d'origine quand ils ont découvert cet appartement dans un immeuble d'exception construit en 1936 par l'architecte d'origine hongroise, Jorge Kálnay, auteur de plusieurs bâtiments emblématiques de la capitale. L'édifice possède toute la noblesse de l'architecture des années 1930, avec des matériaux et des finitions raffinés, un hall en marbre uruguayen. Ils ont laissé intacte la distribution de l'appartement, se contentant de restaurer les portes et le parquet en chêne, et de décaper les ferrures géométriques. L'intérieur est aménagé avec un ensemble de pièces soigneusement choisies qui reflètent la passion des maîtres de maison pour les voyages et l'art argentin du 20ᵉ siècle. Les sculptures et le mobilier des années 1920 à 1970 s'harmonisent parfaitement avec les espaces austères conçus par Kálnay.

RIGHT:
View of the living room. Photograph of Jorge Luis Borges by Annemarie Heinrich (a German photographer who settled in Argentina) and 1940 carpet by the firm Jansen (a furnishings company based in Paris); the "Arquero" (archer) sculpture (1920) is by an unknown Uruguayan artist.

FOLLOWING DOUBLE PAGE:
Living room and study. On the cupboard on the left, a sculpture of a head by Argentinian sculptor Carmen Portela (1930); ottoman in the centre designed by Edward Wombly.

RECHTS:
Im Wohnzimmer ein Foto von Jorge Luis Borges, aufgenommen von Annemarie Heinrich, einer deutschstämmigen, nach Argentinien ausgewanderten Fotografin, ein Teppich von Maison Jansen (1940), einer Ausstatterfirma in Paris, sowie die Skulptur „Arquero" (Bogenschütze) eines unbekannten uruguayischen Künstlers von 1920.

20 FOLGENDE DOPPELSEITE:
Wohnzimmer und Arbeitsraum. Auf dem Möbelstück links ein Porträt der argentinischen Bildhauerin Carmen Portela (1930) und in der Mitte eine von Edward Wombly entworfene Ottomane.

À DROITE :
Dans le séjour, un portrait de Jorge Luis Borges par Annemarie Heinrich (photographe argentine d'origine allemande), un tapis de la maison de décoration parisienne Jansen (1940) et une sculpture de 1920, « Arquero » (L'Archer), d'un artiste uruguayen anonyme.

DOUBLE PAGE SUIVANTE :
Le séjour et le bureau. Sur le meuble à gauche, une tête de la sculptrice argentine Carmen Portela (1930). Au premier plan, un lit de repos dessiné par Edward Wombly.

LEFT PAGE:
Argentinian Art Deco armchairs upholstered in foal hide and table. On the left, a drawing by Argentinian artist Roberto Aizenberg. On the right, a drawing by Mariette Lydis (1950), a French high society portraitist who settled in Argentina.

ABOVE RIGHT:
In the background, an American piano designed for the 1939 New York World's Fair, and a painting entitled "El Caldén" (1989) by Argentinian artist Nicolás García Uriburu.

BELOW RIGHT:
Bathroom faced in travertine stone with oak-veneered door; 1950s washbasin and chair attributed to Charlotte Perriand.

LINKE SEITE:
Mit Fohlenleder bezogene argentinische Art-déco-Sessel und Tischchen. Links eine Zeichnung des argentinischen Künstlers Roberto Aizenberg, rechts ein Werk der französischen High-Society-Porträtistin Mariette Lydis (1950), die sich in Argentinien niederließ.

RECHTS OBEN:
Im Hintergrund ein für die New Yorker Weltausstellung von 1939 entworfenes amerikanisches Klavier und das Gemälde „El Caldén" (1989) des argentinischen Malers Nicolás García Uriburu.

RECHTS UNTEN:
Das mit Travertin ausgekleidete Badezimmer hat eine Tür mit Eichenholzfurnier, ein Waschbecken aus den 1950er-Jahren und einen Charlotte Perriand zugeschriebenen Stuhl.

PAGE DE GAUCHE :
Fauteuils argentins en cuir de poulain et guéridon Art Déco. À gauche, un dessin au crayon de l'artiste argentin Roberto Aizenberg. À droite, un dessin de Mariette Lydis (1950), une portraitiste de la haute société française émigrée en Argentine.

À DROITE, EN HAUT :
Au fond, un piano américain conçu pour l'Exposition universelle de New York en 1939 et une toile de l'artiste argentin Nicolás García Uriburu intitulée « El Caldén » (1989).

À DROITE, EN BAS :
La salle de bains en travertin. Porte plaquée en chêne, lavabo des années 1950 et chaise attribuée à Charlotte Perriand.

CASA KÁLNAY / RETIRO, BUENOS AIRES

ABOVE LEFT:
Bedroom with 1940s chest of drawers with ivory knobs, a 1950 Fontana Arte Italian mirror above.

BELOW LEFT:
Kitchen corner: on the metal and glass fittings designed by Kálnay, a 1930s surgeon's tray and bakelite tray.

RIGHT PAGE:
Bar with 1930s North American sculptures: "Woman" (allegory of theatre); cocktail shaker and a horse's head.

LINKS OBEN:
Im Schlafzimmer eine Kommode mit Elfenbeinknöpfen (1940er-Jahre), der italienische Spiegel (1950) darüber stammt von Fontana Arte.

LINKS UNTEN:
In einer Ecke der Küche stehen auf dem von Kálnay entworfenen Möbelstück aus Metall und Glas ein Tablett für chirurgisches Besteck aus den 1930er-Jahren und ein Tablett aus Bakelit.

RECHTE SEITE:
In der Bar sind nordamerikanische Skulpturen aus den 1930er-Jahren zu sehen: mujer (eine Frauengestalt als Allegorie des Theaters), darunter ein Pferdekopf sowie ein Cocktailshaker.

À GAUCHE, EN HAUT :
Dans la chambre, la commode aux poignées en ivoire, au dessus un miroir italien de Fontana Arte (1950).

À GAUCHE, EN BAS :
Dans un coin de la cuisine, sur le meuble en métal et verre dessiné par Kálnay, un plateau chirurgical des années 1930 et un plateau en bakélite.

PAGE DE DROITE :
Sur le bar, des sculptures américaines des années 1930 : une femme (allégorie du théâtre) et une tête de cheval. Shaker américain des années 1930.

CASA KÁLNAY / RETIRO, BUENOS AIRES

LEFT PAGE:
Bedroom: the backboard and wall have matching lozenge motifs; 1930s Argentinian-design stool.

RIGHT PAGE:
Entrance hall in Uruguay marble with enamelled steel and glass wall lamp designed by Kálnay.

LINKE SEITE:
Im Schlafzimmer harmonieren das Kopfteil des Bettes und die Wand aufgrund ihrer rhombenförmigen Muster. Der Schemel aus den 1930er-Jahren ist argentinisches Design.

RECHTE SEITE:
Wandlampe aus emailliertem Stahl mit einer Glaskugel – nach einem Entwurf von Jorge Kálnay – an der Wand des mit uruguayischem Marmor verkleideten Eingangsbereichs.

PAGE DE GAUCHE :
Dans la chambre, la tête de lit et les murs sont ornés de losanges. Tabouret argentin des années 1930.

PAGE DE DROITE :
Dans le hall d'entrée en marbre uruguayen, une applique en verre et acier émaillé de Jorge Kálnay.

28

Entrance hall of the building: black Belgian marble counter and behind it a glass board with the residents' names.

Vestibül im Eingangsbereich des Gebäudes mit der Pförtnerloge aus schwarzem belgischem Marmor, dahinter eine Glasscheibe mit den Namen der Bewohner.

Le hall d'entrée de l'immeuble avec un comptoir en marbre noir belge. Derrière, un tableau en verre avec les noms des habitants.

30

CASA KÁLNAY / RETIRO, BUENOS AIRES

JUAN GATTI

RETIRO, BUENOS AIRES

After many years abroad, cult art director Juan Gatti has rediscovered Buenos Aires. As a graphic designer he brought a new aesthetic style to Pedro Almodóvar's movies and has worked as a graphic designer, artistic director and photographer for luxury brands such as Sybilla, Chloé, Karl Lagerfeld, Loewe and many others. "I fell in love with the city," he tells us from his 1930s apartment in Plaza San Martín. At his home, where picture windows provide postcard-style views of iconic city features such as the Kavanagh Building, the church of the Holy Sacrament, the port and the jacaranda trees in Plaza San Martín, Gatti welcomes friends from all over the world. For the reconstruction of his apartment he engaged the architects Carlos Rivadulla and Claudia Conde Grand, who lent the rooms a certain clarity and a modern, classical feel. Juan Gatti's extensive trawling of flea markets and a neutral palette have done the rest. "I like American and Scandinavian furniture of the 1950s. My dream has always been to have a playboy-style apartment like those created by legendary Argentinian cartoonist Guillermo Divito," he confides with a certain sophisticated humour.

LEFT PAGE:
Living room with staircase leading to Juan Gatti's bedroom. Hanging from the ceiling, a mobile by Alexander Calder.

LEFT:
General view. The velvet curtains are used to divide the study and the bedroom from the living room.

LINKE SEITE:
Das Wohnzimmer mit der zum Schlafzimmer führenden Treppe. Von der Decke hängt ein Mobile von Alexander Calder herab.

LINKS:
Gesamtansicht innen. Durch die Samtvorhänge lassen sich Arbeitszimmer und Schlafzimmer vom Wohnzimmer trennen.

PAGE DE GAUCHE :
Le séjour, avec l'escalier qui monte à la chambre. Suspendu au plafond, un mobile d'Alexander Calder.

À GAUCHE :
Vue d'ensemble de l'appartement. Les rideaux en velours permettent de séparer le bureau et la chambre de la salle de séjour.

Der Star-Designer und Fotograf mit Kultstatus, der die Filmplakate für Pedro Almodóvar entwirft und für Luxusmarken wie Sybilla, Chloé, Karl Lagerfeld oder Loewe tätig ist, feierte nach Jahren der Trennung ein Wiedersehen mit Buenos Aires. „Ich liebe die Stadt", tönt es aus seinem Apartment aus den 1930er Jahren an der Plaza San Martín. Aus den Fenstern seines Hauses, wo Gatti seine Freunde aus aller Welt empfängt, hat man eine herrliche Aussicht auf einige Ikonen der Stadt, etwa das Kavanagh-Gebäude, die Basilica del Santísimo Sacramento, den Hafen oder die Jacarandas der Plaza San Martín. Für den Umbau seiner Wohnung engagierte Juan Gatti die Architekten Carlos Rivadulla und Claudia Conde Grand, die für eine moderne klassische Note und für die Klarheit der Räume sorgten. Streifzüge Juan Gattis durch die Flohmärkte und eine neutrale Palette taten das Übrige. „Mir gefallen die nordamerikanischen und skandinavischen Möbel der 1950er-Jahre. Eigentlich habe ich mir immer ein Apartment im Playboy-Stil wie bei Guillermo Divito, dem Helden der argentinischen Comics, gewünscht", gesteht Gatti verschmitzt.

Créateur de l'esthétique graphique des films de Pedro Almodóvar, directeur artistique, graphiste et photographe de couturiers et de marques prestigieuses tels que Sybilla, Chloé, Karl Lagerfeld ou Loewe, Juan Gatti a retrouvé Buenos Aires après des années d'absence. « J'en suis tombé amoureux », déclare-t-il depuis son appartement situé dans un édifice des années 1930 où il reçoit ses amis du monde entier. Il a confié sa restructuration aux architectes Carlos Rivadulla et Claudia Conde Grand qui ont rendu les pièces plus claires et leur ont apporté une touche à la fois classique et moderne. Les fenêtres donnent sur l'immeuble Kavanagh, l'église du Santísimo Sacramento, le port et les jacarandas de la place San Martín en contrebas. Pour le décor, Gatti a opté pour une palette neutre et ses trouvailles dans les marchés aux puces. « J'aime les meubles américains et scandinaves des années 1950 », confie-t-il, ajoutant avec humour : « J'ai toujours rêvé d'avoir une garçonnière de playboy dans le style de celles des bandes dessinées de Guillermo Divito, le légendaire illustrateur argentin. »

Above the Scandinavian-design sideboard, a photograph of Milla Jovovich by Peter Lindbergh and a 1970s ceiling lamp.

RIGHT PAGE:

Seen through the window is the Kavanagh Building, constructed in 1934. Foal-hide rug and 1960s Finn Juhl-style armchairs.

LINKE SEITE:

Über dem Sideboard im skandinavischen Stil ziehen eine von Peter Lindbergh aufgenommene Fotografie von Milla Jovovich und eine Hängelampe aus den 1970er-Jahren den Blick auf sich.

RECHTE SEITE:

Durch das Wohnzimmer-fenster sieht man das 1934 errichtete Kavanagh-Gebäude. Auf dem Boden ein Teppich aus Fohlenfell und Armsessel aus den 1960er-Jahren im Stil von Finn Juhl.

PAGE DE GAUCHE :

Au-dessus du buffet scandinave, un portrait de Milla Jovovich par Peter Lindbergh et un luminaire des années 1970.

PAGE DE DROITE :

Par la fenêtre du séjour, on aperçoit le Kavanagh, construit en 1934. Tapis en poulain, fauteuils des années 1960 dans le style Finn Juhl.

34

JUAN GATTI / RETIRO, BUENOS AIRES

LEFT PAGE:
Living room with Italian-design sofa by the marble fireplace. On one side, a nest of tables by an unknown designer purchased by Juan Gatti in the Dorrego flea market.

ABOVE RIGHT:
Over the fireplace, a photograph by Peter Lindbergh and 1930s glassware. "Womb" armchair and ottoman by Eero Saarinen.

BELOW RIGHT:
Detail of 1930s glassware and photo from Gatti's collection.

LINKE SEITE:
Das Sofa im italienischen Stil steht im Wohnzimmer gegenüber dem Marmorkamin. Seitlich sind ineinanderschiebbare Beistelltischchen eines unbekannten Designers zu sehen, die Juan Gatti auf dem Flohmarkt von Dorrego kaufte.

RECHTS OBEN:
Auf dem Kaminsims eine Fotografie von Peter Lindbergh und Kristallobjekte aus den 1930er-Jahren. „Womb"-Sessel und Ottomane von Eero Saarinen.

RECHTS UNTEN:
Detailaufnahme von Kristallobjekten aus den 1930er-Jahren und eine Fotografie aus der Sammlung des Hausherrn.

PAGE DE GAUCHE :
Le séjour. Devant la cheminée en marbre, un canapé de style italien. Sur le côté, des tables gigognes, d'un designer anonyme, que Juan Gatti a trouvées sur le marché aux puces de Dorrego.

À DROITE, EN HAUT :
Sur la cheminée, une photo de Peter Lindbergh et des vases des années 1930. Fauteuil et ottomane « Womb » d'Eero Saarinen.

À DROITE, EN BAS :
Vases en cristal des années 1930 et photo de la collection de Juan Gatti.

JUAN GATTI / RETIRO, BUENOS AIRES

ABOVE LEFT:
Desk with copies of the literary magazine "Sur" founded by Victoria Ocampo in 1931 and 1930s glass vase from Gatti's collection.

BELOW LEFT:
Study with 1960 Finn Juhl-style armchair. The velvet curtains are used to divide the different spaces.

RIGHT PAGE ABOVE:
Gatti's bedroom situated on a balcony area overlooking the living room. On the bed, an otter-skin throw and on the wall photos from his collection of 1930s nudes.

RIGHT PAGE BELOW:
Living room with a carpet designed by Emilio Pucci in 1960; a chair from the "Aluminium Group" by Charles and Ray Eames.

LINKS OBEN:
Auf einer Ablage ein Exemplar der 1931 von Victoria Ocampo gegründeten literarischen Zeitschrift „Sur" und eine Vase aus den 1930er-Jahren aus der Sammlung von Juan Gatti.

LINKS UNTEN:
Im Arbeitszimmer Lehnsessel aus den 1960er-Jahren im Stil Finn Juhls. Samtvorhänge trennen die verschiedenen Räume.

RECHTE SEITE OBEN:
Juans Schlafzimmer auf der Galerie über dem Wohnzimmer. Eine Decke aus Nutriafell liegt auf dem Bett, an der Wand steht auf einem Brett eine Sammlung von Aktaufnahmen aus den 1930er-Jahren.

RECHTE SEITE UNTEN:
Im Wohnbereich ein von Emilio Pucci 1960 entworfener Teppich sowie ein Bürostuhl aus der „Aluminium Group" von Charles und Ray Eames.

À GAUCHE, EN HAUT :
Sur une table basse, des numéros de la revue littéraire « Sur », fondée par Victoria Ocampo en 1931 et un vase des années 1930.

À GAUCHE, EN BAS :
Dans le bureau, un fauteuil des années 1960, dans le style Finn Juhl. Des rideaux en velours divisent les espaces.

PAGE DE DROITE, EN HAUT :
La chambre, située sur une mezzanine donnant sur le séjour. Plaid en loutre sur le lit et, au mur, des nus des années 1930.

PAGE DE DROITE, EN BAS :
Le salon, avec un tapis dessiné par Emilio Pucci dans les années 1960. Un fauteuil du « Aluminium Group » de Charles et Ray Eames.

JUAN GATTI / RETIRO, BUENOS AIRES

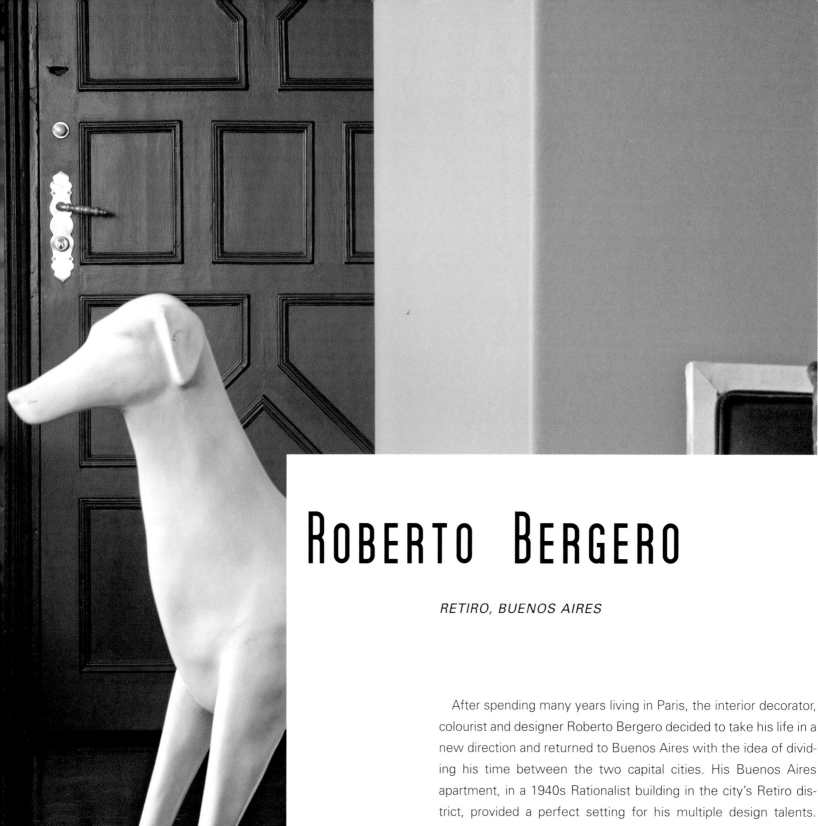

ROBERTO BERGERO

RETIRO, BUENOS AIRES

After spending many years living in Paris, the interior decorator, colourist and designer Roberto Bergero decided to take his life in a new direction and returned to Buenos Aires with the idea of dividing his time between the two capital cities. His Buenos Aires apartment, in a 1940s Rationalist building in the city's Retiro district, provided a perfect setting for his multiple design talents. Audacious combinations of styles and colour were the basic criteria for the "staging" of the interior. A selection of furniture and sculptures bought on impulse have created a home that is a true reflection of its owner. Bergero is not afraid of mixing styles. In fact, in his opinion "the solution to increasing the sense of space is not to unify everything with a coat of white paint. On the contrary, I feel that the use of colours and special effects can generate new planes that always improve the perception of an environment." The result is an impactful mix of baroque, kitsch and vintage with touches of 1940s French theatricality staged in a way that is revealing of the owner's strong personality.

LEFT PAGE:

"Not so much a major piece of restoration, more a work of reclamation," explains Bergero. In front of the original door a 1930s plaster dog from the city's Dorrego flea market.

RIGHT:

A mixture of styles has been Bergero's key approach in transforming his new apartment. He is seen here with his dogs Octavia and Carlota.

LINKE SEITE:

„Es war keine große Umgestaltung nötig, sondern vielmehr eine Wiederherstellung," erklärt Bergero. Vor der Originaltür die Gipsfigur eines Hundes aus den 1930er-Jahren vom Dorrego-Flohmarkt in Buenos Aires.

RECHTS:

Roberto Bergero griff zu einer bunten Stilmischung, um sein neues Apartment einzurichten. Hier ist der Hausherr mit seinen Hündinnen Octavia und Carlota zu sehen.

PAGE DE GAUCHE :

« J'ai surtout cherché à retrouver l'esprit d'origine de l'appartement », explique Bergero. Devant la porte d'entrée d'origine, un chien en plâtre des années 1930 chiné sur le marché d'antiquités de Dorrego, à Buenos Aires.

À DROITE :

Le maître de maison, avec ses chiennes Octavia et Carlota.

41

Nach vielen Jahren in Paris beschloss der Dekorateur, Maler und Designer Roberto Bergero, nach Buenos Aires zurückzukehren und seine Zeit zwischen den beiden Hauptstädten zu teilen. Seine Vielseitigkeit kommt in seinem Apartment in Buenos Aires zum Ausdruck, das innerhalb des Retiro-Viertels in einem dem Rationalismus der 1940er-Jahre verpflichteten Gebäude liegt. Kühne Stil- und Farbkombinationen dienten als Grundlage der Inneneinrichtung. Mit spontan gekauften Möbeln und Skulpturen hat der Hausherr die Wohnung nach seinem Geschmack eingerichtet. Vor Stilmischungen fürchtet sich Bergero jedenfalls nicht. Er meint, dass „der Raum nicht größer wirkt, wenn man alles weiß streicht. Ich finde im Gegenteil, dass Farben und spezielle Effekte ganz neue Flächen hervorbringen können, die stets die Wahrnehmung eines Ambientes verbessern." Das Resultat ist eine eindrucksvolle Mischung aus barocken, französischen, Kitsch- und Vintage-Elementen der 1940er-Jahre. Die einer Theaterproduktion ähnelnde Inszenierung offenbart die starke Persönlichkeit des Hausherrn.

Après de longues années à Paris, le décorateur, coloriste et designer Roberto Bergero, pris d'une envie de changement, a décidé de rentrer à Buenos Aires et de partager son temps entre les deux capitales. Fort de ses multiples talents, il s'est attelé à la réfection d'un appartement situé dans un immeuble rationaliste des années 1940, près de la gare du Retiro. Sa décoration est le fruit d'audacieuses combinaisons de styles et de couleurs, agrémentées par une sélection de meubles et de sculptures achetés sur des coups de cœur. Il faut dire que Bergero ne craint pas les mélanges. Pour lui, « On cherche souvent à agrandir une pièce en la peignant tout en blanc. Au contraire, l'utilisation de couleurs et d'effets texturaux peuvent créer de nouvelles perspectives qui améliorent toujours la perception des espaces. » Il en résulte un métissage franco, baroque et théâtral, parsemé de touches des années 1940, qui reflète bien la forte personnalité du maître de maison.

Various styles live side by side in the living room: Jean-Michel Frank armchair, the famous "La Chaise" Eames chair and "Tulip" chairs by Eero Saarinen. The table in coral-red plaster and glass was made by Bergero.

Im Salon finden sich verschiedene Stilarten nebeneinander: ein Sessel von Jean-Michel Frank, der berühmte Eames-Stuhl „La Chaise" und die „Tulip"-Stühle von Eero Saarinen. Der korallenrot gestrichene und mit einer Glasplatte versehene Stucktisch wurde von Bergero gefertigt.

Un savant mélange de styles : fauteuil de Jean-Michel Frank, la célèbre « Chaise » des Eames, sièges « Tulip » d'Eero Saarinen. La table, en plâtre peint couleur corail et plateau de verre, est de Bergero.

42

ROBERTO BERGERO / RETIRO, BUENOS AIRES

LEFT PAGE:
On the French sideboard, a sculpture by Alexander Calder. In the foreground, a resin sculpture of a giant hand by French artist César.

ABOVE RIGHT:
A patchwork mosaic of old tiles from various sources enliven the kitchen walls. Table and "Side Chairs" by Harry Bertoia for Knoll.

BELOW RIGHT:
In the bedroom, the sculptural plaster light fitting and painting are both by Bergero. The large French mask has been painted white.

LINKE SEITE:
Auf der französischen Kommode steht eine Skulptur von Alexander Calder. Im Vordergrund „La main géante" (die Riesenhand), ein aus Gießharz gestaltetes Werk des französischen Bildhauers César.

RECHTS OBEN:
Patchwork aus antiken Kacheln unterschiedlicher Herkunft, ein belebendes Element an der Küchenwand. Dazu ein Tisch und „Side Chairs", von Harry Bertoia für Knoll entworfen.

RECHTS UNTEN:
Dominierende Elemente dieses Zimmers sind ein Gemälde und eine Lampe aus Gips mit skulptiertem Fuß, beide von Bergero geschaffen. Die französische Maske wurde weiß bemalt.

PAGE DE GAUCHE :
Sur la commode française revisitée par Bergero, une sculpture de Calder. Au premier plan, « La Main géante », une œuvre en résine du sculpteur César.

À DROITE, EN HAUT :
Sur les murs de la cuisine, un patchwork de carreaux de ciment d'origines diverses. Table et chaises « Side Chairs » de Harry Bertoia pour Knoll.

À DROITE, EN BAS :
Dans la chambre, une toile inspirée par Picasso et des lampes sculptures en plâtre de Bergero. Le masque en fonte repeint en blanc provient d'un ancien portail français.

ROBERTO BERGERO / RETIRO, BUENOS AIRES

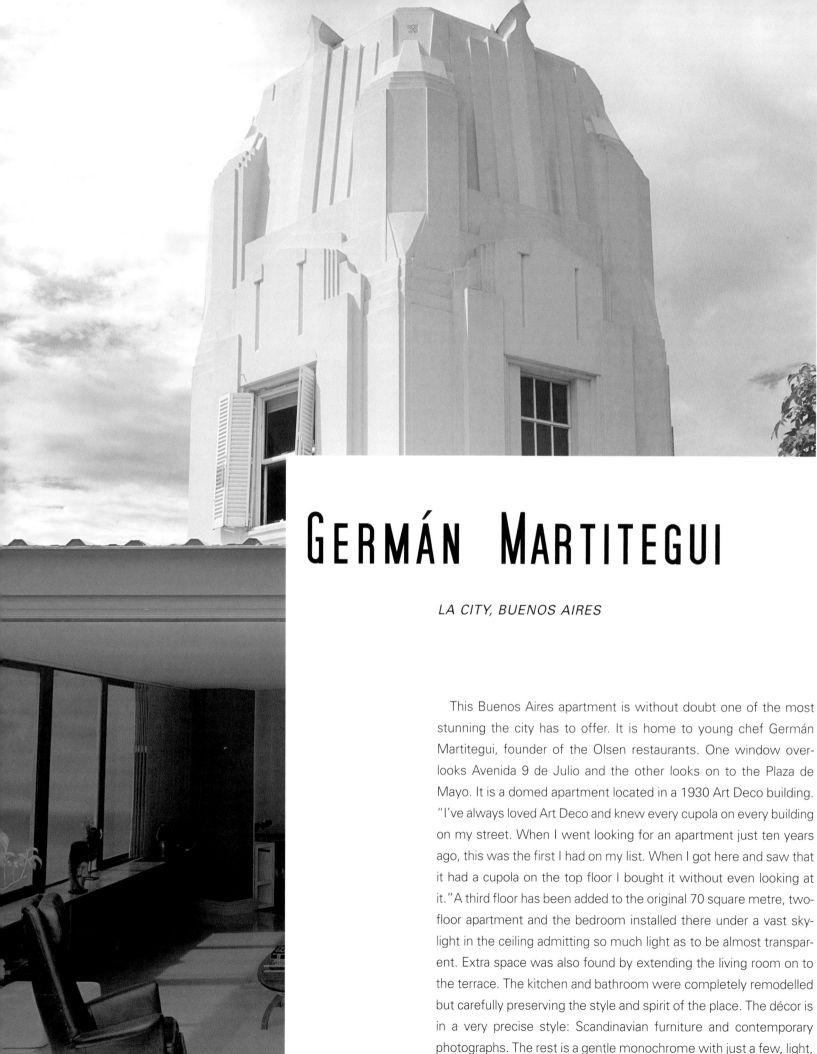

GERMÁN MARTITEGUI

LA CITY, BUENOS AIRES

This Buenos Aires apartment is without doubt one of the most stunning the city has to offer. It is home to young chef Germán Martitegui, founder of the Olsen restaurants. One window over-looks Avenida 9 de Julio and the other looks on to the Plaza de Mayo. It is a domed apartment located in a 1930 Art Deco building. "I've always loved Art Deco and knew every cupola on every building on my street. When I went looking for an apartment just ten years ago, this was the first I had on my list. When I got here and saw that it had a cupola on the top floor I bought it without even looking at it." A third floor has been added to the original 70 square metre, two-floor apartment and the bedroom installed there under a vast sky-light in the ceiling admitting so much light as to be almost transpar-ent. Extra space was also found by extending the living room on to the terrace. The kitchen and bathroom were completely remodelled but carefully preserving the style and spirit of the place. The décor is in a very precise style: Scandinavian furniture and contemporary photographs. The rest is a gentle monochrome with just a few, light, isolated touches of colour. The resulting style is impressive.

Germán Martitegui, der Gründer der Olsen-Restaurants, wohnt im vornehmsten Viertel von Buenos Aires. Von einem Fenster blickt er auf die Avenida 9 de Julio, vom anderen auf die Plaza de Mayo. Es handelt sich um ein Apartment in einem Art-déco-Kuppelbau von 1930. „Mir hat Art déco immer gefallen, und ich kannte die Kuppeln aller Häuser in meiner Straße. Als ich vor zehn Jahren eine Wohnung suchte, war dieses Apartment das erste auf meiner Liste. Als ich merkte, dass es in der letzten Etage eine Kuppel gab, habe ich es fast unbesehen gekauft." Die ursprünglich zweigeschossige, 70 Quadratmeter umfassende Wohnung wurde um eine dritte Etage für das Schlafzimmer erweitert, das durch ein Oberlicht erhellt wird. Noch mehr Platz wurde durch die Erweiterung des Wohnzimmers um die Terrasse gewonnen. Die Küche und das Bad erfuhren eine Erneuerung, doch unter Berücksichtigung von Stil und Charakter der ursprünglichen Räumlichkeiten. Das Interieur ist stilistisch präzise definiert: skandinavische Möbel und zeitgenössische Fotografie. Dabei ist alles, von leichten Farbtupfen abgesehen, monochrom gehalten.

L'appartement du jeune chef Germán Martitegui, fondateur des restaurants Olsen, est sans doute le lieu d'où l'on a la plus belle vue sur Buenos Aires : une fenêtre donne sur l'avenue 9 de Julio ; une autre sur la Plaza de Mayo. Il est situé dans un immeuble Art Déco de 1930. « J'ai toujours aimé ce style et connaissais toutes les coupoles dans ma rue. Quand j'ai cherché un appartement il y a dix ans, cet édifice était le premier sur ma liste. Quand j'ai vu qu'il y avait une coupole, je l'ai acheté les yeux fermés », se souvient-il. L'appartement de 70m² comptait initialement deux étages. Il en a ajouté un troisième pour abriter sa chambre, percée d'une faîtière pour contempler le ciel de son lit. Il a également gagné de l'espace en prolongeant le séjour sur la terrasse. La cuisine et la salle de bains ont été repensées en préservant l'essence du lieu. La décoration répond à un style bien précis : meubles nordiques et photos contemporaines. Partout, une douce monochromie est rehaussée ici et là de quelques touches de couleur. L'effet est puissant.

ABOVE LEFT:
Due to the height of the building, Martitegui's apartment offers an exceptional panoramic view over the district.

BELOW LEFT:
The stairs seen from the first floor. Martitegui bought the "AIR" wall relief at the Vanves flea market in Paris; lower down is a sculpture made by Martitegui himself from old ships' turbines.

RIGHT PAGE ABOVE:
The entrance hall to the building with its wealth of marble and bronze still in its original condition, providing a perfect visual record of Buenos Aires's past.

RIGHT PAGE BELOW:
Another view of the entrance hall. Its elegant fittings are a breath of fresh air amidst the chaotic remodelling that has afflicted most of the buildings in the surrounding area.

LINKS OBEN:
Von der Terrasse des Apartments hat man einen wunderbaren Panoramablick auf das Viertel.

LINKS UNTEN:
Die vom Obergeschoss der Wohnung hinabführende Treppe mit der Wandinstallation „AIR", ein Zufallsfund Martiteguis auf dem Flohmarkt von Vanves in Paris; weiter unten eine Skulptur, die er selbst als Hobbykünstler aus alten Schiffsturbinen gestaltete.

RECHTE SEITE OBEN:
Die reich mit Marmor und Bronze ausgestattete Eingangshalle des Gebäudes präsentiert sich im Originalzustand, ein seltenes Beispiel für das historische Erbe von Buenos Aires.

RECHTE SEITE UNTEN:
Eine andere Ansicht des Eingangsbereichs, dessen elegante Elemente wie eine erholsame Atempause inmitten all der Veränderungen wirken, die die meisten Gebäude der Umgebung erfahren haben.

À GAUCHE, EN HAUT :
Du fait de la hauteur de l'immeuble, l'appartement de Martitegui jouit d'une exceptionnelle vue panoramique sur le quartier.

À GAUCHE, EN BAS :
L'escalier qui relie les étages. Une applique « AIR », achetée par Martitegui au marché aux puces de Vanves, à Paris, et une sculpture qu'il a réalisée lui-même avec des turbines de bateau.

PAGE DE DROITE, EN HAUT :
L'entrée de l'immeuble, avec ses marbres et ses bronzes d'origine, exemple parfait du patrimoine architectural de Buenos Aires.

PAGE DE DROITE, EN BAS :
Une autre vue du hall d'entrée. La noblesse des matériaux offre un répit dans le chaos des restaurations douteuses subies par la plupart des autres immeubles du quartier.

50

ABOVE LEFT:
On the wood-and-glass table in the centre are opalescent glass vases and a vintage ceramic dish bought in the San Telmo, the most famous flea market in Buenos Aires.

BELOW LEFT:
As a chef, the nerve centre of Martitegui's penthouse is the kitchen. Picture by Sergio Avello and Scandinavian-design lamp.

RIGHT PAGE ABOVE:
First-floor living room: gunpowder picture by Argentinian artist Tomás Espina. The leather sofa, table and lamps are some of the many finds Martitegui has made in his frequent trawling of flea markets across the world. The "LCW"-chairs are by Charles and Ray Eames.

RIGHT PAGE BELOW:
On the lower floor, the living room merges with the terrace. On the guatambú wood sideboard are Zulu masks and a ceramic by Dominic Bromley, bought in London. Outside, the purpose-built teak furniture and stools are by Sori Yanagi reproduced by Vitra.

LINKS OBEN:
Auf dem Tisch aus Holz und Glas stehen Vasen aus Milchglas und Kristall sowie ein Keramikteller vom berühmtesten Flohmarkt von Buenos Aires in San Telmo.

LINKS UNTEN:
Die Küche ist das Herzstück im Apartment von Germán Martitegui, denn hier kocht der Chef mit Leidenschaft! Das Bild stammt von Sergio Avello, und die Tischlampe ist ein skandinavisches Design.

RECHTE SEITE OBEN:
Im Salon ein mit verbranntem Schießpulver geschaffenes Gemälde des argentinischen Künstlers Tomás Espina. Das Ledersofa, der Tisch und die Lampen sind einige der zahlreichen Zufallsfunde, die der Hausherr von Flohmärkten weltweit zusammengetragen hat. Die „LCW"-Stühle stammen von Charles und Ray Eames.

RECHTE SEITE UNTEN:
Der Salon im unteren Geschoss der Wohnung geht in die Terrasse über. Auf dem Sideboard aus guatambú-Holz stehen Zulu-Masken und in London gekaufte Keramikvasen von Dominic Bromley. Auf der Terrasse finden sich maßgefertigte Teakholzmöbel und Hocker von Sori Yanagi, die von Vitra neu aufgelegt wurden.

À GAUCHE, EN HAUT :
Sur la table basse en bois et verre, des vases en opaline et en cristal ainsi qu'une assiette en céramique achetés sur le célèbre marché aux puces de San Telmo.

À GAUCHE, EN BAS :
La cuisine est le centre névralgique de l'appartement, le jeune chef pouvant y donner libre cours à sa passion. Tableau de Sergio Avello et lampe scandinave.

PAGE DE DROITE, EN HAUT :
Dans le salon du premier étage, un tableau en poudre calcinée de l'artiste argentin Tomás Espina. Le canapé en cuir, la table et les lampes sont quelques-unes des trouvailles du maître de maison qui adore chiner dans des marchés aux puces aux quatre coins du monde. Les chaises « LCW » sont de Charles et Ray Eames.

PAGE DE DROITE, EN BAS :
À l'étage inférieur, le salon se prolonge sur la terrasse. Sur le buffet en bois guatambú, des masques zoulous et des potiches en céramique de Dominic Bromley achetées à Londres. À l'extérieur, des meubles en teck réalisés sur mesure et des tabourets de Sori Yanagi pour Vitra.

LEFT PAGE:
Bedroom: the hexagonal skylight dominates the ceiling. The photo on the wall is by Miguel Rothschild.

RIGHT PAGE:
Dining room with "Naturaleza geométrica" painting by Fabián Burgos. 1950s oak-topped metal table. Danish chairs by Hans J. Wegner and lamp by George Nelson.

LINKE SEITE:
Im Schlafzimmer zieht das alles beherrschende hexagonale Oberlicht die Aufmerksamkeit auf sich. Die Fotografie an der Wand ist ein Werk von Miguel Rothschild.

RECHTE SEITE:
Das Bild im Speisezimmer mit dem Titel „Naturaleza geométrica" ist von Fabian Burgos. Der Tisch mit Eichenplatte stammt aus den 1950er-Jahren. Dänische Stühle von Hans J. Wegner und darüber eine Lampe von George Nelson.

PAGE DE GAUCHE :
Dans la chambre, une grande lucarne hexagonale percée dans le toit. Sur le mur du fond, une photographie de Miguel Rothschild.

PAGE DE DROITE :
Dans la salle à manger, une toile de Fabián Burgos, « Naturaleza geométrica ». Une table métallique avec un plateau en chêne des années 1950. Chaises danoises de Hans J. Wegner. Plafonnier de George Nelson.

52

GERMÁN MARTITEGUI / LA CITY, BUENOS AIRES

MARTÍN CHURBA &
MAURO BERNARDINI

COLEGIALES, BUENOS AIRES

The textile artist Martín Churba, creator of the Tramando brand, shares this apartment with the architect Mauro Bernardini. Both men are outstanding exponents of Argentina's new trend-setting generation. The interior style of their home, which occupies the top two floors of a modern building, is characterised by handcrafted designs and a mixture of unusual accessories. It is a style without preconceptions, where everything appears spontaneous with no other agenda than reflecting the owners' taste. "We try to bring value to what society throws out and we put maximum effort into it." The ingenious creations that are the result live side by side in this home with designer and handcrafted furniture. Churba's concept is to create for a purpose using reclaimed materials. It is a philosophy that has led to an imaginative recycling of materials discarded by industry and to the creation of textile cooperatives providing work for the unemployed. He also works with native peoples in the north of Argentina, who bring quality craftsmanship to his avant-garde designs. Churba's home is a true reflection of his creative genius.

Der Textilkünstler Martín Churba, Urheber der Marke Tramando, teilt diesen Wohnsitz mit dem Architekten Mauro Bernardini. Bcide sind perfekte Vertreter der neuen Generation von Trendsettern in Argentinien. Die Wohnung auf den zwei letzten Etagen eines modernen Gebäudes ist geprägt von handwerklichem Design und einer Mischung verblüffender Accessoires. Die ausgefallene Dekoration scheint vorurteilslos nur den Geschmack der Hausherren zu reflektieren. „Wir wollen das, was die Gesellschaft wegwirft oder missachtet, aufwerten. Darauf verwenden wir unsere Energie." Neuschöpfungen stehen hier neben bekannten Designermöbeln und Spezialanfertigungen. Churba versucht durch Wiederverwertung, kreative Kräfte zu mobilisieren. Daher hat er sich dem erfinderischen Recycling von Industrieabfällen zugewandt und mit Arbeitslosen eine Textilgenossenschaft gegründet. Auch Indios aus dem Norden von Argentinien bezieht er ein, sie bringen ihre handwerklichen Techniken in die avantgardistischen Schöpfungen ein. Sein Zuhause ist das Spiegelbild seines kreativen Genius.

L'artiste textile Martín Churba, créateur de la marque Tramando dont la boutique est devenue un véritable lieu de pèlerinage, partage cet appartement avec l'architecte Mauro Bernardini. Ces deux parfaits représentants de la nouvelle génération qui créé les tendances en Argentine, ont aménagé leur espace, qui occupe les deux derniers étages d'un immeuble moderne, avec leur design artisanal et un assortiment d'accessoires surprenants. Dans leur décor sans préjugé, tout paraît spontané et sans autre prétention que de refléter le goût des propriétaires. « Nous cherchons à valoriser ce que la société rejette et à le retravailler au maximum », explique Churba. Ses créations ingénieuses cohabitent avec des meubles signés et artisanaux. Son concept : la création basée sur la récupération. Il recycle ainsi des matériaux textiles ou plastiques délaissés par l'industrie et a fondé une coopérative textile avec des groupes de chômeurs. Il travaille également avec les Indiens du nord de l'Argentine qui apportent leurs techniques artisanales à ses créations avant-gardistes. Son appartement est le reflet de son génie créatif.

ABOVE LEFT:
In Churba's boutique Tramando, scraps of fabric are given a new lease of life as clothing and household objects.

BELOW LEFT:
On the kitchen worktop, Churba has transformed a wooden bat into an original, decorative fruit dish by piercing it with chopsticks.

RIGHT PAGE ABOVE:
The staircase leads to the bedroom. The "BKF" leather armchair, also known internationally as the "Hardoy" or "Butterfly" chair, was designed in 1938 by Argentinian architects Antonio Bonet, Jorge Ferrari Hardoy and Juan Kurchan.

RIGHT PAGE BELOW:
Living room: curtains designed by Mauro Bernardini; pouffe and rug by Martín Churba; seats and the "LCW" chairs by Charles and Ray Eames.

LINKS OBEN:
Im Tramando-Shop werden Stoff- und Wollreste zu neuem Leben erweckt, um daraus Kleidung und Haushaltsgegenstände zu machen.

LINKS UNTEN:
Auf der Arbeitsfläche in der Küche liegt ein dekorativer Holzschläger, den Martín mit Essstäbchen spickte und so in eine originelle Fruchtschale verwandelte.

RECHTE SEITE OBEN:
Die Treppe führt ins Schlafzimmer. Der Ledersessel „BKF", international auch als „Hardoy" oder „Butterfly Chair" bekannt, wurde 1938 von den Argentiniern Antonio Bonet, Jorge Ferrari Hardoy und Juan Kurchan entworfen.

RECHTE SEITE UNTEN:
Von Mauro Bernardini konzipierte Vorhänge im Salon, Puff und Teppich von Martín Churba, dazu von Charles und Ray Eames entworfene „LCW"-Stühle.

À GAUCHE, EN HAUT :
Dans la boutique Tramando, on donne une nouvelle vie aux chutes de tissu en créant des vêtements et des objets pour la maison.

À GAUCHE, EN BAS :
Sur le plan de travail de la cuisine, une coupe de fruits originale créée avec une raquette et des baguettes chinoises.

PAGE DE DROITE, EN HAUT :
L'escalier mène à la chambre. Le fauteuil en cuir « BKF », connu internationalement sous le nom « Hardoy » ou « Butterfly Chair », a été dessiné en 1938 par les Argentins Antonio Bonet, Jorge Ferrari Hardoy et Juan Kurchan.

PAGE DE DROITE, EN BAS :
Dans le salon, des rideaux conçus par Mauro Bernardini. Pouf et tapis de Martín Churba, les chaise « LCW » de Charles et Ray Eames.

LEFT PAGE:
Churba's work table with its everyday work objects reflects the owner's personality and profession. Churba describes it as "made beautiful by its technology, utility and craftsmanlike finish."

RIGHT PAGE:
The mood in the bathroom is simple and playful – unusual domestic objects bring a sense of everyday fun.

LINKE SEITE:
Der Arbeitstisch von Martín Churba und seine Utensilien spiegeln den Beruf und die Persönlichkeit des Hausherrn wider, der feststellt: „Ich setze auf Technologie, Nützlichkeit und handwerkliche Verarbeitung."

RECHTE SEITE:
Im Badezimmer, wo eine schlichte und fröhliche Atmosphäre herrscht, finden sich unterschiedliche Gegenstände für den alltäglichen Gebrauch.

PAGE DE GAUCHE :
La table de travail de Martín Churba, qui reflète bien son travail et sa personnalité. « Je parie sur la technologie, la fonctionnalité et les finitions artisanales. »

PAGE DE DROITE :
Dans la salle de bains, simple et amusante, un assortiment d'objets quotidiens.

58

FRANCIS MALLMANN

LA BOCA, BUENOS AIRES

Francis Mallmann is something of an Argentinian trademark. As a chef, Mallmann has been responsible for raising culinary art to a new level in Argentina and has become the country's representative abroad. And he's a trend setter… Mallmann is a tireless traveller but during the short spells he spends in Buenos Aires, he likes to lay anchor at his house and his restaurant in La Boca, an Italian immigrant district just a few minutes from the city centre. The three-storey house, built in 1920, is surrounded by balconies and has river views, high ceilings and is steeped in the grace and splendour of that period. Here Mallmann passes his time among his books and films and enjoys visits from his neighbours. "There is a certain madness, charm and diversity about La Boca," explains Mallmann. "And it's a real neighbourhood. There are grocery stores, hairdressers. My neighbour Helena comes to take my dog Luna for a walk every day; there's the bar on the corner where I have breakfast with the locals. For me what is magical is living in a building with a twelve-cover restaurant operating on the ground floor; it makes me feel as if people are coming to eat at my house."

LEFT PAGE:
The house, painted in different colours, is in keeping with the tradition of this district and is reminiscent of Naples, which is where many of the locals originally came from.

LEFT:
The balconies are typical of the La Boca district and very similar to those found in the south of Italy. Originally, the house was a greengrocer's store.

LINKE SEITE:
Das in verschiedenen Farben gestrichene Haus folgt den Traditionen dieses Viertels, die an Neapel, den Herkunftsort seiner Einwohner, erinnern.

LINKS:
Die charakteristischen Balkone von La Boca, die den süditalienischen stark ähneln. Ursprünglich beherbergte das Haus einen Gemüseladen.

PAGE DE GAUCHE :
La façade, peinte de différentes couleurs, suit la tradition du quartier qui rappelle Naples, la ville d'origine des habitants de La Boca.

À GAUCHE :
Typiques de La Boca, les balcons évoquent l'Italie du Sud. Le bâtiment abritait autrefois un marchand de légumes.

Man könnte sagen, dass Francis Mallmann für Argentinien ein Markenzeichen ist. Er führte die hohe Schule der Kochkunst in diesem Land ein, vertrat sie im Ausland und wirkte als Trendsetter. Francis reist viel, und in der kurzen Zeit, die er in Buenos Aires verbringt, lebt er wenige Minuten vom Zentrum entfernt in seinem Wohnhaus mit Restaurant im italienischen Immigrantenviertel La Boca. Das dreigeschossige Haus von 1920 ist mit umlaufenden Balkonen ausgestattet; es hat Ausblicke auf den Fluss, hohe Decken und die mit Grazie gepaarte Erhabenheit seiner Bauzeit. Hier lebt der Koch zwischen Büchern und Filmen und den Besuchen seiner Nachbarn. „La Boca ist verrückt, zauberhaft, kontrastreich", sagt Francis, „und dabei ganz vorstädtisch. Es gibt Läden und Friseure und meine Nachbarin Helena, die jeden Tag Luna, meine Hündin, zum Spazierengehen abholt, ebenso die Bar an der Ecke, wo ich mit Kumpels frühstücke. Für mich hat es einen eigenen Zauber, in einem Gebäude samt eigenem Restaurant mit zwölf Plätzen im Erdgeschoss zu leben, weil ich das Gefühl habe, dass die Leute mich persönlich besuchen."

On peut dire que Francis Mallmann est une marque déposée argentine. Ce chef a introduit l'art de la cuisine dans notre pays et fait connaître la nôtre au reste du monde. Il crée la tendance. Voyageur infatigable, quand il rentre à Buenos Aires, c'est à la Boca, un quartier d'immigrés italiens à quelques minutes du centre-ville, qu'il prend ses quartiers. Sa maison/restaurant de trois étages, construite en 1920, est ceinte de balcons d'où l'on voit le fleuve. Avec ses hauts plafonds, elle possède toute la grâce et la majesté des années folles. Mallmann y passe ses journées à lire, à regarder des films, à recevoir ses voisins. « La Boca est un vrai quartier, un peu fou, plein de charme et de contrastes. Il y a des épiceries, des coiffeurs, ma voisine Helena qui vient promener Luna, ma chienne, le bar du coin où je vais déjeuner avec les habitués … Je trouve magique de vivre dans un bâtiment dont le rez-de-chaussée est un restaurant de douze couverts. C'est comme si j'accueillais les gens chez moi. »

ABOVE LEFT:
Francis Mallmann on the first floor of his house. Behind him, the door to the living room where he keeps his film collection, beyond which is the kitchen.

BELOW LEFT:
The balcony with wooden seating designed by Mallmann and inspired by old Scandinavian benches that converted into beds; Moroccan plant holders.

RIGHT PAGE:
Mallmann's small living room and study on the second floor, located in the angle forming the corner of the building, contains large-scale furniture and objects. On the left-hand wall is an English needle-point tapestry by Robert Adam.

LINKS OBEN:
Francis Mallmann in der ersten Etage seines Hauses. Hinter ihm die Tür, die zu dem Raum führt, in dem er seine Sammlung von Filmen aufbewahrt, dahinter liegt die Küche.

LINKS UNTEN:
Der Balkon mit Sitzbänken, die von alten skandinavischen Möbeln inspiriert und von Francis entworfen sind. Sie lassen sich zu Betten umwandeln. An der Brüstung marokkanische Blumentöpfe.

RECHTE SEITE:
Im kleinen Wohn- und Arbeitszimmer Mallmanns in der zweiten Etage wurden großformatige Möbel in die Ecknische plaziert. An der linken Wand ein englischer Wandteppich von Robert Adam.

À GAUCHE, EN HAUT :
Francis Mallmann au premier étage. Derrière lui, la porte donnant sur sa filmothèque et sa cuisine.

À GAUCHE, EN BAS :
Les banquettes en bois du balcon, dessinées par Mallmann, s'inspirent de vieux bancs scandinaves qui se convertissaient en lits. Pots de fleurs marocains.

PAGE DE DROITE :
Dans cette petite pièce d'angle, qui sert de salon et de bureau, Mallmann a choisi de ne mettre que des meubles et des objets de grande taille. Sur le mur de gauche, une tapisserie anglaise de Robert Adam.

FRANCIS MALLMANN / LA BOCA, BUENOS AIRES

LEFT PAGE:
In the bathroom, adjoining the dressing room, are textiles from India and Bhutan. In the dressing room is a work bench designed by Ricardo Paz and Francis Mallmann.

ABOVE RIGHT:
The staircase that connects the three floors of the house. Seen hanging, a series of "Watergraphs" by Martin Summers, which originally decorated Mallmann's Patagonia West restaurant in Westhampton (United States).

BELOW RIGHT:
The master bedroom on the third floor, with beams painted black like those in Paris bistros, and oak floor. Over the table, an etching by Giovanni Battista Piranesi.

LINKE SEITE:
Im Bad neben dem Ankleidezimmer eine Auswahl von Stoffen aus Indien und Bhutan. Im Ankleidezimmer steht ein von Ricardo Paz und Francis Mallmann entworfener Arbeitstisch.

RECHTS OBEN:
Die Treppe verbindet die drei Geschosse des Hauses miteinander. An der Wand des Treppenaufgangs die Serie von „Watergraphs", eine Arbeit von Martin Summers, die ursprünglich Mallmanns Restaurant Patagonia West in Westhampton (USA) dekorierte.

RECHTS UNTEN:
Das Hauptschlafzimmer im dritten Geschoss mit den schwarz gestrichenen Deckenbalken, die an Pariser Bistros erinnern, und dem Bodenbelag aus Eichenholz. Über dem Tisch hängt ein Stich von Giovanni Battista Piranesi.

PAGE DE GAUCHE :
Dans la salle de bains attenante au dressing, des tissus d'Inde et du Bhoutan. Dans le dressing, la table a été dessinée par Ricardo Paz et Francis Mallmann.

À DROITE, EN HAUT :
La cage d'escalier. Au mur, une série de « Watergraphs », de Martin Summers, qui décorait autrefois un autre restaurant de Mallmann, Patagonia West, à Westhampton (États-Unis).

À DROITE, EN BAS :
La chambre principale, au dernier étage, avec un parquet en chêne et des poutres apparentes peintes en noir à la manière des bistrots parisiens. Au dessus de la table de chevet, une gravure de Piranèse.

FRANCIS MALLMANN / LA BOCA, BUENOS AIRES

66

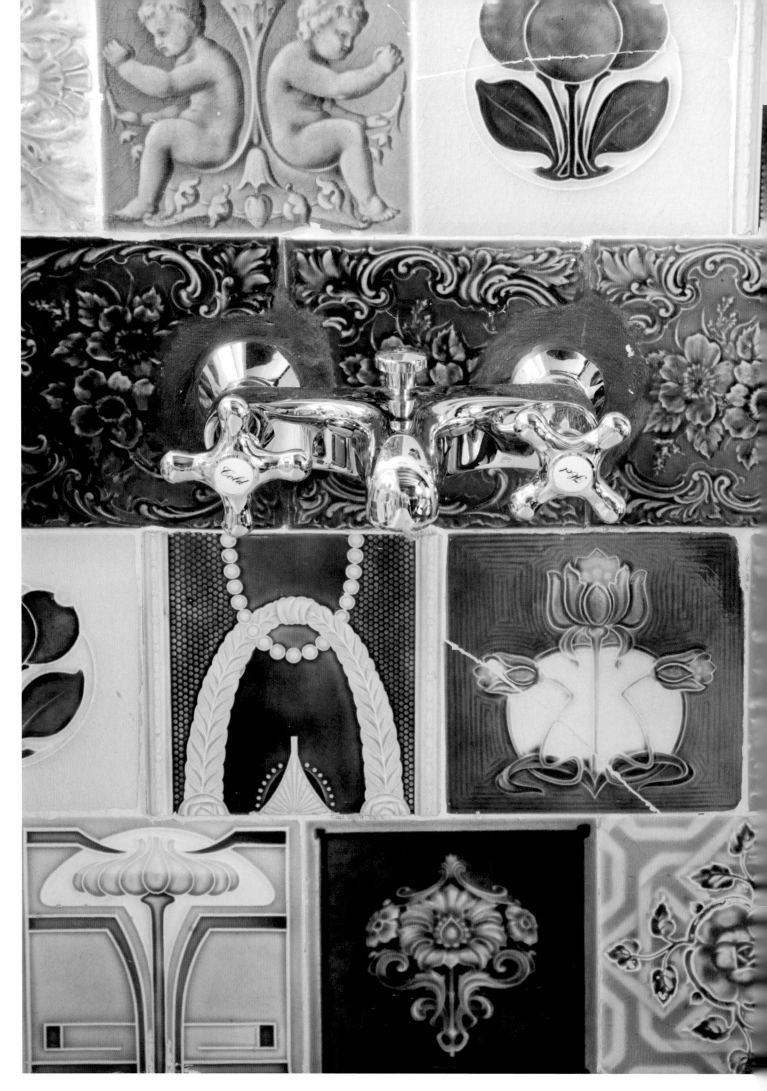

FRANCIS MALLMANN / LA BOCA, BUENOS AIRES

RICARDO CINALLI

CENTRO, BUENOS AIRES

Ricardo Cinalli, a well-known Argentinian artist with an international career, was inspired by his restoration work on the "Resurrezione" (Resurrection) at Terni Cathedral in Italy to produce the frescoes in this apartment that he recently chose to be his pied-à-terre in Buenos Aires. The building is of great historical importance, being considered one of the best examples of Art Deco architecture in the city. The apartment was restored and improved by Mario Salcedo. It was possible to preserve the original materials and retain the layout of the rooms; the walls were covered in a collage of mirrored glass and have now become a perfect backdrop for Cinalli's work. A faithful reflection of his passion, his paintings provide a setting that evokes a dream-like world akin to the world of mythology. The décor here is insignificant and the few pieces of furniture in the apartment are individual items and not intended as adornment but as objects one can live alongside. In this apartment the principal common denominator is the owner's sensibility.

LEFT PAGE:
The frescoes are a reinterpretation of the neoclassical style, inhabited by dream-like figures.

LEFT:
In every corner of the apartment a monochromatic harmony of golds, greys and white prevails.

LINKE SEITE:
Die Fresken sind eine Neuinterpretation des klassizistischen Stils und werden von Figuren bevölkert, die einem Traum entstiegen scheinen.

LINKS:
In allen Räumen herrscht eine gedämpfte Farbgebung in Grau, Weiß und Gold.

PAGE DE GAUCHE :
Réinterprétation du style néoclassique, les fresques sont peuplées de personnages semblant sortis d'un rêve.

À GAUCHE :
Dans tout l'appartement règne une harmonie tri-chromatique de tons dorés, gris et blanc.

Inspiriert von seiner Restaurierung der „Resurrezione" (Auferstehungsszene) in der Kathedrale von Terni in Italien, schuf Ricardo Cinalli, ein namhafter argentinischer Maler von internationalem Ruf, die Fresken dieses Apartments, das er sich gerade als *Pied-à-terre* in Buenos Aires gewählt hatte. Das Gebäude, in dem die Wohnung liegt, ist historisch sehr bedeutend, gilt es doch als eines der besten Beispiele der Art-déco-Architektur in der Stadt. Das Apartment wurde von Mario Salcedo restauriert und gestaltet, der die ursprünglichen Materialien konservierte und die Aufteilungen bewahrte. Die Wände erhielten eine Collage aus Spiegeln, vor allem aber wurden sie zur perfekten Leinwand, auf der sich das Werk Cinallis entfaltet. Seine Kompositionen, Spiegel seines künstlerischen Empfindens, sind Inszenierungen einer traumhaften Welt, die sich der Mythologie nähert. Die Ausstattung folgt keiner bestimmten Richtung, da die wenigen Möbel Unikate sind und keine dekorative, sondern eine rein praktische Funktion erfüllen sollen. Der größte gemeinsame Nenner ist hier die Sensibilität des Besitzers.

Pour son pied-à-terre à Buenos Aires, Ricardo Cinalli, artiste de renommée internationale, s'est inspiré de sa restauration de la fresque monumentale, la « Resurrezione » (Résurrection), réalisée dans la cathédrale de Terni, en Italie. L'appartement, situé dans un immeuble chargé d'histoire (c'est un des plus beaux fleurons de l'architecture Art Déco de la capitale), a été remodelé et mis en valeur par Mario Salcedo. Ce dernier a conservé les matériaux d'origine ainsi que la distribution des pièces dont les murs, quand ils ne sont pas tapissés d'un collage de miroirs, offrent un support parfait aux peintures de Cinalli. Fidèle reflet de sa passion, celles-ci mettent en scène des compositions oniriques proches de la mythologie. Ici, point de décoration. Les rares meubles sont des pièces uniques et ne jouent qu'un rôle fonctionnel. Partout, le principal dénominateur commun est la sensibilité du propriétaire.

ABOVE LEFT:
The building's main entrance with its Art Deco, wrought-iron door conveys an infallible sense of style. It is one of the outstanding buildings of that period.

BELOW LEFT:
Passageways of undeniable elegance with chequered tile floors and materials that still glow with their original beauty and have been preserved in outstanding condition.

RIGHT PAGE:
In the apartment's entrance hall, drawings inspired by Picasso are reflected in the mirrored cupboard door.

LINKS OBEN:
Die mit Art-déco-Motiven verzierte schmiedeeiserne Eingangstür strahlt den unverwechselbaren Stil des Gebäudes aus, das eines der schönsten Bauwerke seiner Zeit in Buenos Aires darstellt.

LINKS UNTEN:
Vestibül von großer Eleganz mit schachbrettartig verlegtem Fliesenboden und Materialien, die in ihrer ursprünglichen Schönheit und in perfektem Zustand erhalten sind.

RECHTE SEITE:
Im Eingangsbereich des Apartments werden Zeichnungen im Stile von Picasso von der Spiegeltür des Schranks reflektiert.

À GAUCHE, EN HAUT :
La porte d'entrée en fer forgé de l'immeuble, ornée de motifs Art Déco. C'est l'un des plus beaux exemples de cette période.

À GAUCHE, EN BAS :
L'élégance incontestable du hall, avec son sol en damier et ses matériaux qui irradient leur beauté d'origine, est conservé dans un parfait état.

PAGE DE DROITE :
Dans le vestibule de l'appartement, des dessins dans le Style de Picasso se reflètent dans la porte en miroir d'une armoire.

RICARDO CINALLI / CENTRO, BUENOS AIRES

PREVIOUS DOUBLE PAGE:
The frescoes portray a mythological world. The vintage, gold, velveteen armchair is from the city's San Telmo antique market.

LEFT PAGE:
Over the day bed, the Cubist-inspired painting "La foresta" is by Cinalli himself.

ABOVE RIGHT:
The 1930s medical table was once used for massage. The chairs and lamp fitting date from the same period.

BELOW RIGHT:
Fresco detail: once again, grey and gold tones that blend with the other elements of the room.

VORIGE DOPPELSEITE:
Die Fresken sind Kompositionen aus einer Welt, die der Mythologie nahesteht. Der Vintage-Sessel aus goldfarbenem Cordsamt stammt vom Antiquitätenmarkt in San Telmo, Buenos Aires.

LINKE SEITE:
Das vom Kubismus inspirierte Bild „La foresta" ist ein Werk von Ricardo Cinalli.

RECHTS OBEN:
Eine zum Tisch umfunktionierte Liege – vielleicht aus einer Praxis der 1930er-Jahre – diente zur Anwendung von Massagen. Die Stühle und die Lampe stammen aus derselben Zeit.

RECHTS UNTEN:
Ausschnitt aus einem Fresko, dessen Grau- und Goldtöne mit den Elementen des Raums harmonieren.

DOUBLE PAGE PRÉCÉDENTE :
Les fresques présentent des visions d'un monde qui évoque la mythologie. Fauteuil vintage en velours côtelé doré provenant du marché d'antiquités de San Telmo, à Buenos Aires.

PAGE DE GAUCHE :
Au-dessus de la dormeuse, « La foresta », une œuvre de Ricardo Cinalli d'inspiration cubiste.

À DROITE, EN HAUT :
Une table de massage des années 1930. Les fauteuils et le lustre sont de la même époque.

À DROITE, EN BAS :
Détails d'une fresque, dans les mêmes tons gris et or que tout le reste de l'appartement.

75

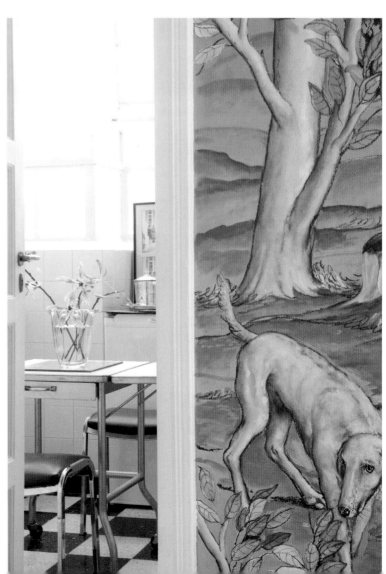

RICARDO CINALLI / CENTRO, BUENOS AIRES

Cinalli has taken a humorous approach with the impalas – both found in Buenos Aires, but in different places and at different times – mounting one on wheels and surrounding the other with a sunburst of mirrored glass.

Cinalli verlieh den Antilopen – zwei Zufallsfunde, die er an zwei verschiedenen Orten in Buenos Aires erwarb – eine humoristische Note; die eine erhielt Räder, die andere einen Heiligenschein aus Spiegelglas.

Cinalli a trouvé ses deux impalas empaillés à des époques et dans des lieux différents. Il leur a apporté sa touche d'humour : l'un est monté sur roue, l'autre couronné d'une auréole en miroir.

76

RICARDO CINALLI / CENTRO, BUENOS AIRES

ABOVE LEFT:
The bedroom houses an old glass display cabinet filled with linen and curiosities.

BELOW LEFT:
View into the bathroom: the classic-design fittings are original and the walls are covered in vintage glass reclaimed from other buildings.

RIGHT PAGE:
"The bedroom is my theatre of sleep, the set that prepares me for rest" – in a custom-made captain's bed.

LINKS OBEN:
Die antike Glasvitrine enthält Wäsche und Kuriositäten.

LINKS UNTEN:
Blick in das Bad klassischen Zuschnitts mit sanitären Einrichtungen aus der Bauzeit. Die Wände sind mit originalen Glasfliesen ausgekleidet, die aus Abrisshäusern stammen.

RECHTE SEITE:
„Das Schlafzimmer ist mein Traumtheater, das Szenario, das mich für die Ruhe vorbereitet." Maßgefertigtes Polsterbett.

À GAUCHE, EN HAUT :
Dans la chambre, une ancienne vitrine remplie de linge et de curiosités.

À GAUCHE, EN BAS :
Vue de la salle de bains, avec ses sanitaires classiques d'origine et ses murs tapissés de carreaux en verre peint récupérés dans des immeubles en démolition.

PAGE DE DROITE :
« La chambre est le théâtre de mes rêves, la scène qui me prépare au repos. » Lit capitonné réalisé sur mesure.

RICARDO CINALLI / CENTRO, BUENOS AIRES

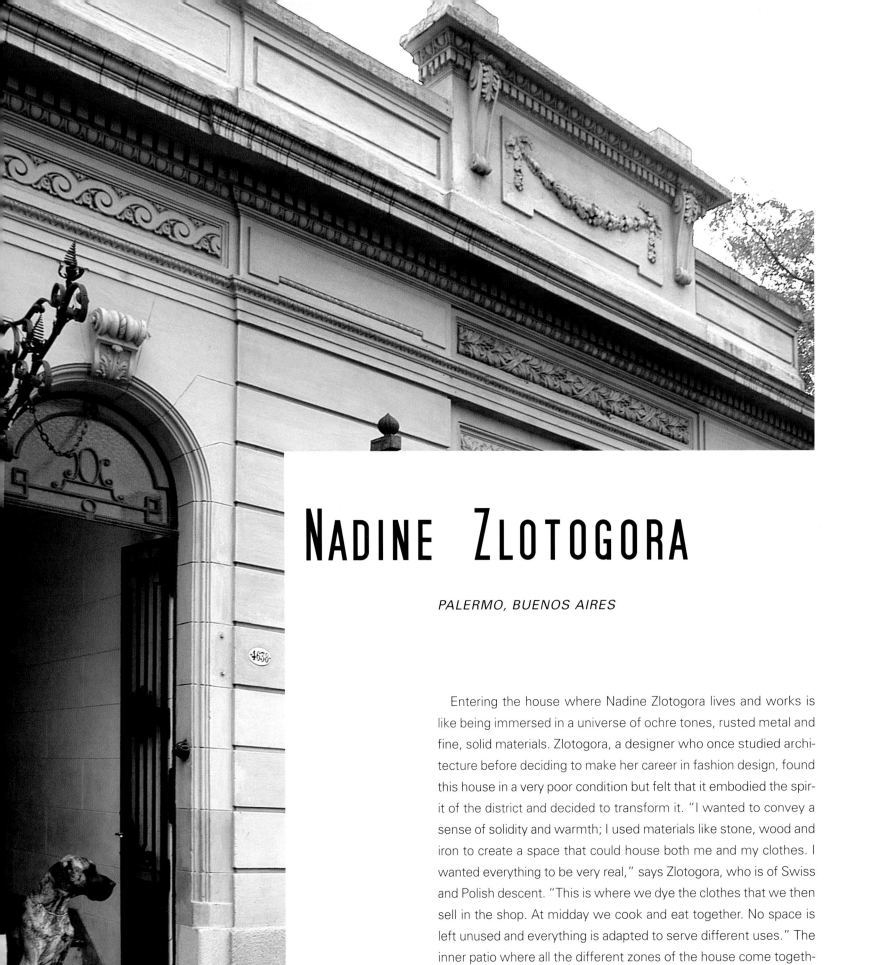

NADINE ZLOTOGORA

PALERMO, BUENOS AIRES

Entering the house where Nadine Zlotogora lives and works is like being immersed in a universe of ochre tones, rusted metal and fine, solid materials. Zlotogora, a designer who once studied architecture before deciding to make her career in fashion design, found this house in a very poor condition but felt that it embodied the spirit of the district and decided to transform it. "I wanted to convey a sense of solidity and warmth; I used materials like stone, wood and iron to create a space that could house both me and my clothes. I wanted everything to be very real," says Zlotogora, who is of Swiss and Polish descent. "This is where we dye the clothes that we then sell in the shop. At midday we cook and eat together. No space is left unused and everything is adapted to serve different uses." The inner patio where all the different zones of the house come together is the connecting link and the owner's favourite spot. "In winter it can sometimes be cold in this patio, but it is light and airy, which is the most important thing." As for the colours … they are the same as she uses in her designs – she describes them as "dirty; once they were different but they have become like this with age."

LEFT PAGE:
Façade of Nadine's house and shop – characteristic of many Buenos Aires neighbourhoods, with a typical early 20th-century layout on a narrow, deep plot.

RIGHT:
Nadine Zlotogora with her dog Vito, a tiger-striped Great Dane.

LINKE SEITE:
Fassade des Wohn- und Geschäftshauses von Nadine: Der Bau mit einem typischen Grundriss vom Anfang des 20. Jahrhunderts auf einem schmalen und lang gestreckten Grundstück ist für die Stadtviertel von Buenos Aires charakteristisch.

RECHTS:
Nadine Zlotogora mit Vito, ihrer großen getigerten dänischen Dogge.

PAGE DE GAUCHE :
La façade de la maison boutique, caractéristique des quartiers populaires de Buenos Aires, avec un plan typique du début du 20e siècle : étroit et tout en longueur.

À DROITE :
Nadine Zlotogora et Vito, son danois au pelage tigré.

In das Wohn- und Geschäftshaus von Nadine Zlotogora einzutreten gleicht dem Eintauchen in ein Universum aus Ockerfarben und rostigem Eisen im Kontrast zu edlen Materialien. Das Haus ist in einem schlechten Zustand, hat aber die vornehme Aura des Viertels. Es wurde von der Designerin selbst umgebaut, die einmal Architektur studiert hatte, sich aber dafür entschied, Mode zu entwerfen. „Ich wollte Qualität und Wärme vermitteln und verwendete Materialien wie Stein, Holz oder Eisen, um eine Umgebung für mich und meine Kleider zu schaffen. Alles sollte sehr real sein", stellt die Designerin mit Schweizer und polnischen Wurzeln fest. „Hier wird die Kleidung gefärbt, die wir im Laden verkaufen. Mittags kochen und essen wir alle zusammen. Es gibt keinen ungenutzten Raum, und alles richtet sich nach den verschiedenen Funktionen. Der Patio ist Kommunikationszentrum und Lieblingsaufenthaltsort der Hausherrin. „Im Winter ist es manchmal kalt in diesem Patio, aber es gibt Licht und Luft, was für mich am wichtigsten ist." Dazu kommen ihre Farben, die sie „schmutzig" nennt, „weil ihr Urzustand mit der Zeit verblichen ist."

La maison boutique de Nadine Zlotogora, au cœur de Palermo, est un univers de tons terre, de fer oxydé, de matières nobles. Quand elle l'a découverte, la bâtisse était dans un état déplorable mais lui rappelait le quartier de son enfance. Nadine, qui a des origines suisses et polonaises, a d'abord fréquenté la faculté d'architecture avant d'opter pour le stylisme. Elle a transformé la structure en « cherchant à la rendre chaleureuse, authentique et robuste avec des matières comme la pierre, le bois et le fer, afin qu'elle puisse nous accueillir, moi et mes créations. C'est ici que l'on teint et coud les vêtements que l'on vend ensuite dans la partie boutique. Aucun espace n'est perdu. À midi, on cuisine et on déjeune tous ensemble. » Le patio, sur lequel convergent toutes les pièces, est le centre de communication et le lieu préféré de la styliste. « En hiver, il peut faire froid, mais il est lumineux et aéré » … et plein de couleurs, les mêmes qu'elle utilise pour ses vêtements et qu'elle définit comme « passées, qui ont eu une autre vie et que le temps a patiné ».

ABOVE LEFT:
The kitchen: majolica ware by artist Ana Manghi; 1970s lampshade and cement worktop painted by Nadine with inlaid majolica tiles.

BELOW LEFT:
On the bathroom wall, small fragments of old painted glass that look like bubbles and shower curtain made of organza and shirt fabric.

RIGHT PAGE:
Inner patio with staircase leading to Nadine's bedroom, decorated with violets. On the table loom, a textile designed by Nadine.

LINKS OBEN:
In der Küche Majolika-Kacheln der Künstlerin Ana Manghi, eine Deckenlampe aus den 1970er-Jahren und ein Spültisch mit Zementplatte, mit von Nadine eingelegten farbigen Majolika-Kacheln verziert.

LINKS UNTEN:
An der Wand des Badezimmers tanzen kleine grüne Glasfragmente wie perlende Luft- und Wasserblasen; der Duschvorhang besteht aus Organza und Hemdblusenstoff.

RECHTE SEITE:
Die mit Töpfen blühender Alpenveilchen geschmückte Treppe im Patio führt in Nadines Wohnung. Auf dem Tisch ein von Nadine entworfenes Webstück.

À GAUCHE, EN HAUT :
Dans la cuisine, des carreaux en majolique de l'artiste Ana Manghi, un lustre des années 1970 et un plan de travail en ciment peint par Nadine et incrusté de carreaux en céramique.

À GAUCHE, EN BAS :
Sur le mur de la salle de bains, des morceaux de verre peints, imitant des bulles. Rideau de douche en organdi et batiste.

PAGE DE DROITE :
Dans le patio, l'escalier qui mène à la chambre de Nadine est orné de violettes. Sur la table, un tissage artisanal, œuvre de la maîtresse de maison.

NADINE ZLOTOGORA / PALERMO, BUENOS AIRES

PREVIOUS PAGE LEFT:
Inner courtyard: rusted masks detail on the wall – a reference to the past, as are Zlotogora's own romantic creations.

PREVIOUS PAGE RIGHT:
In the patio, a wire mannequin with dyed fabric samples for future collections hanging to dry in the sun, and the door leading to the shop at the front.

RIGHT:
The kitchen: furniture rescued from Nadine's grandparents' house and from skips in the street and then renovated and painted by her.

VORIGE SEITE LINKS:
Im Patio beschwören drei verrostete Masken an der Wand vergangene Zeiten, wie das auch die romantischen Kreationen der Designerin tun.

VORIGE SEITE RECHTS:
Im Patio eine Schneiderpuppe aus Draht, auf die kleine gefärbte Stoffproben für die künftigen Kollektionen zum Trocknen aufgehängt werden. Dahinter der zur Straßenfront des Geschäfts führende Korridor.

86

RECHTS:
In der Küche stehen Möbel, die Nadine aus dem Haus ihrer Großeltern und vom Sperrmüll gerettet, selbst repariert und gestrichen hat.

PAGES PRÉCÉDENTES, À GAUCHE :
Dans le patio central, des masques oxydés sont accrochés au mur. Comme les créations romantiques de la styliste, ils renvoient au passé.

PAGES SUIVANTES, À DROITE :
Dans le patio, un mannequin en fil de fer sur lesquels on fait sécher au soleil des essais de teinture pour la prochaine collection, et le couloir menant à la rue.

À DROITE :
Dans la cuisine, des meubles que la styliste a trouvés dans la rue ou récupérés chez ses grands-parents, et qu'elle a ensuite repeints.

NADINE ZLOTOGORA / PALERMO, BUENOS AIRES

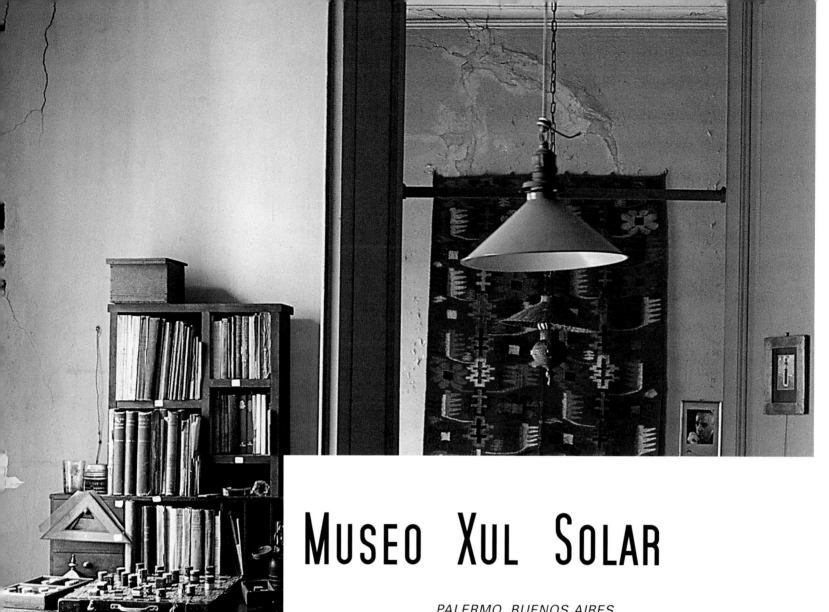

Museo Xul Solar

PALERMO, BUENOS AIRES

"A man versed in every discipline, curious for all that is arcane, progenitor of texts, languages, utopias, mythologies, guest of hell and of heaven, creator of *panajedrez* and astrologist…. Xul Solar is one of the most singular events in our history." This is how Jorge Luis Borges described his friend Xul Solar. Preserved as part of the museum that now houses his work, the house where the artist lived with his wife, mother and aunt was the meeting place of the local avant-garde during the 1930s. Borges, Victoria Ocampo and Adolfo Bioy Casares, among others, would spend hours there while their host coined words for his invented languages or elucidated the rules of *panajedrez*, the board game he created. Picked out in contrast against the pale and esoteric pinks and blues of the walls are the pieces of furniture he constructed, strange plants, religious objects, revamped musical instruments and a library containing over 3,500 volumes. Permeated by the artist's eccentric and refined spirit, his house remains intact.

LEFT PAGE:
View from the main living room into the bedroom. On the desk constructed by Xul Solar is one of the games he invented.

LEFT:
In the centre a draughts board camping table modified by Xul Solar, and a watercolour from his "Zodiac" series.

LINKE SEITE:
Blick vom Wohn- ins Schlafzimmer. Auf dem von Xul Solar geschaffenen Schreibpult eines der von ihm erfundenen Spiele.

LINKS:
Im Zentrum ein Klapptisch mit dem von Solar modifizierten Damebrett und ein Aquarell aus der „Zodiac"-Serie.

PAGE DE GAUCHE :
La chambre à coucher vue depuis le salon principal. Sur le bureau construit par Xul Solar, un jeu de son invention.

À GAUCHE :
Au centre, une table de camping avec un damier « modifié » par Solar. Au mur, une aquarelle de sa série « Zodiaque ».

„Ein auf allen Gebieten beschlagener Mann, hungrig nach verborgenem Wissen, Vater der Schrift, der Sprachen, der Utopien, der Mythologien, dessen Herz Himmel und Hölle kennt, Schöpfer des *panajedrez* und perfekter Astrologe. Xul Solar ist eines der außergewöhnlichsten Ereignisse unserer Geschichte." So beschrieb Jorge Luis Borges seinen Freund Xul Solar. Das Haus, in dem der Künstler mit seiner Frau, seiner Mutter und seiner Tante lebte, ist heute Teil des Museums, in dem sein Werk aufbewahrt wird. In den 1930er-Jahren war es Mittelpunkt der Avantgarde in Buenos Aires. Borges, Victoria Ocampo und Adolfo Bioy Casares verbrachten hier neben anderen viele Stunden, während der Herr des Hauses Worte für erfundene Sprachen kreierte oder die Regeln des *panajedrez* erklärte, eines von ihm erdachten Spiels. Selbst gefertigte Möbel, mysteriöse Pflanzen, religiöse Gegenstände, umgestaltete Musikinstrumente und die Bibliothek mit über 3.500 Bänden heben sich von dem blassen und esoterischen Rosa und Himmelblau der Wände ab. Das völlig intakte Haus atmet noch immer seinen exzentrisch-feinsinnigen Geist.

« Versé dans toutes les disciplines, curieux de tous les domaines, maître en écritures, en langages, en utopies, en mythologies, hôte des enfers et des cieux, auteur *panajédriste* et astrologue parfait, Xul Solar est l'un des événements les plus singuliers de notre histoire. » C'est ainsi que Jorge Luis Borges décrivait son ami. Devenue partie du musée qui abrite ses œuvres, la maison où l'artiste vivait avec sa femme, sa mère et sa tante fut le lieu de réunion de l'avant-garde argentine dans les années 1930. Borges, Victoria Ocampo et Adolfo Bioy Casares, entre autres, y passaient des heures à écouter le maître de maison créer des mots dans des langues de son cru ou leur expliquer les règles du *panajedrez*, un jeu de son invention. Les meubles créés par lui, des plantes ésotériques, des objets religieux, des instruments de musique recyclés et une bibliothèque comptant plus de 3.500 volumes se détachent sur les mystérieux roses et bleus pâles des murs, les mêmes couleurs qu'il utilisait pour ses aquarelles. Imprégnée de son esprit excentrique et raffiné, la demeure reste intacte.

LEFT PAGE:
Panajedrez – a 64-piece board game incorporating elements of astrology and philosophy. Borges and Xul would play for hours at a time.

RIGHT PAGE:
The entrance hall and narrow staircase leading to "la celda" (the cell) – the artist's studio and place of meditation.

LINKE SEITE:
Das panajedrez-Spiel mit 64 der Astrologie und der Philosophie entliehenen Figuren. Borges und Solar spielten es stundenlang.

RECHTE SEITE:
Das Vestibül im Eingangs-bereich und die schmale Treppe zur „la celda" (Zelle), die dem Künstler als Atelier und Meditations-raum diente.

PAGE DE GAUCHE :
Le panajedrez, un jeu de 64 pièces incluant des éléments d'astrologie et de philosophie. Solar et Borges y jouaient des heures durant.

PAGE DE DROITE :
Le hall d'entrée et l'étroit escalier menant à la « la celda » (la celluk), atelier et lieu de méditation de l'artiste.

90

PREVIOUS DOUBLE PAGE, LEFT:
Landing with colour-glazed windows and chequered floor tiles, leading to the kitchen and bathroom.

PREVIOUS DOUBLE PAGE, RIGHT:
Xul Solar's bedroom with windows overlooking the street. On the wall is a rug from Catamarca Province in northwest Argentina. On the right a photo of Xul himself.

ABOVE LEFT:
On the dining-room sideboard is a horn vase with angels and, just visible, a watercolour by Xul from his "Sanmástiles" series.

BELOW LEFT:
Entrance hall, library and tea room. Marionette representation of "death" in the Tarot. The curtains were woven by Xul's wife and disciple, Lita.

RIGHT PAGE:
Corner view with salamander stove and "Victrola" phonograph. On the wall, a "Grafía plastiútil". In the background, a watercolour from Solar's "Sanmástiles" series, painted in 1949.

FOLLOWING DOUBLE PAGE:
Entrance hall and library where tea was taken every day at five in the afternoon; a custom still observed today by those in charge of the house and museum.

VORIGE DOPPELSEITE, LINKS:
Der Durchgang mit farbigen Fensterscheiben und dem Fliesenboden mit Schachbrettmuster, über den man zur Küche und zum Bad gelangt.

VORIGE DOPPELSEITE, RECHTS:
Das Schlafzimmer von Xul Solar mit Fenstern zur Straße. An der Wand ein Teppich aus der Provinz Catamarca. Rechts eine Fotografie von Xul Solar.

LINKS OBEN:
Auf dem Sideboard eine aus Horn geschnitzte und mit Engeln verzierte Blumenvase sowie Teilansicht eines Aquarells von Xul Solar aus der Serie „Sanmástiles".

LINKS UNTEN:
Eingang, Bibliothek, Teesalon mit einem Gerippe aus Holz, das im Tarot als Verkörperung des Todes gilt. Die Vorhänge wurden von Lita, seiner Frau und Schülerin, gewebt.

RECHTE SEITE:
Ecke mit Dauerbrennofen und altem Victrola-Grammofon. An der Wand „Grafía plastiútil". Im Hintergrund ein Aquarell aus der Serie „Sanmástiles" von 1949.

FOLGENDE DOPPELSEITE:
Eingang und Bibliothek, wo jeden Tag nachmittags um fünf Uhr der Tee eingenommen wurde, ein Brauch, der bis heute von den Hütern des Museums und des Hauses beibehalten wird.

DOUBLE PAGE PRÉCÉDENTE, À GAUCHE :
Le couloir menant à la salle de bains et la cuisine, avec des vitres colorées et un sol en damier.

DOUBLE PAGE PRÉCÉDENTE, À DROITE :
La chambre de Solar, dont les fenêtres donnent sur la rue. Au mur, un tapis provenant de la province de Catamarca (nord-ouest de l'Argentine). Sur la droite, un portait de Xul Solar.

À GAUCHE, EN HAUT :
Sur le buffet, un vase en corne sculptée d'anges et, derrière, une autre aquarelle appartenant à la série « Sanmástiles ».

À GAUCHE, EN BAS :
Entrée, bibliothèque et salon de thé. La marionnette représente la carte de la mort au tarot. Les rideaux ont été réalisés par Lita, l'épouse et disciple du maître.

PAGE DE DROITE :
Un coin du salon avec le poêle et un vieux tournedisque. Au dessus, « Grafía plastiútil ». Sur le mur du fond, une aquarelle de 1949, appartenant à la série « Sanmástiles ».

DOUBLE PAGE SUIVANTE :
L'entrée et la bibliothèque où l'on prenait le thé à cinq heures, une tradition qu'entretiennent aujourd'hui les conservateurs du musée et de la maison.

MUSEO XUL SOLAR / PALERMO, BUENOS AIRES

ALAN FAENA

PUERTO MADERO, BUENOS AIRES

Alan Faena's name is inextricably linked with the Faena Hotel + Universe, a hotel that has become an iconic element of the city of Buenos Aires. A highly successful entrepreneur, Faena joined forces with Philippe Starck and Norman Foster to bring the best of international architecture and design to Buenos Aires, producing a fusion with local values that has rekindled the spirit of the city's Belle Époque. His home bears the hallmarks that set the man apart: strength, fantasy and provocativeness. It resembles a stage set where furniture and objects purchased in antique shops are arranged in a spontaneous and eclectic manner. Throughout, an avalanche of materials and styles is unleashed: wood, glass, velvet, silk, animal hide, lace. And while elsewhere it could well have seemed too much, here all these elements have been treated with talent, refinement and even a certain rigour that render them charming. The result is an original interior where everything is the product of an ongoing pursuit of pleasure and harmony. "A house should be emotion" – and Faena breaks all the rules, reinventing the classical bourgeois style in a new and unexpected way.

99

Der Name Alan Faena ist untrennbar mit dem Faena Hotel + Universe verbunden, das bereits zu einer Ikone der Stadt geworden ist. Der erfolgreiche Unternehmer schloss sich mit Philippe Starck und Norman Foster zusammen, um die beste internationale Architektur und das weltweit beste Design nach Buenos Aires zu holen und hier die Belle Époque neu aufleben zu lassen. Sein Haus ist extravagant: Es hat Kraft, ist fantasievoll und provoziert. Die in Antiquitätenläden gekauften Möbel und Objekte wurden spontan und eklektisch angeordnet. Im Wohn- und Schlafzimmer ebenso wie in der Küche und im Bad sind eine Entfesselung von Stilen und eine Lawine von Materialien zu beobachten: Holz, Kristallglas, Samtstoffe, Seide, Felle und Spitzen. Anderswo könnte dies aufdringlich wirken, doch hier sind diese Komponenten mit Talent, Sorgfalt und sogar einer gewissen Strenge behandelt, was sie bezaubernd macht. Das Resultat: ein originelles Wohnhaus, in dem alles der Suche nach Freude und Harmonie entspringt. „Das Haus muss Gefühle auslösen" – Alan bricht die Regeln, indem er eine überraschende Form klassischer Bürgerlichkeit neu erfindet.

Difficile de dissocier le nom d'Alan Faena du Faena Hotel + Universe, devenu un monument emblématique de la ville. Ce brillant entrepreneur s'est associé à Philippe Starck et Norman Foster pour importer le meilleur du design et de l'architecture internationale, la faire fusionner avec les valeurs locales et faire revivre la Belle Époque de Buenos Aires. Sa maison porte l'empreinte qui le distingue : forte, imaginative et provocatrice. C'est une mise en scène où les meubles et les objets chinés chez les antiquaires sont associés de manière spontanée et éclectique. Du séjour à la chambre en passant par la cuisine et la salle de bains, c'est un déferlement de styles et une avalanche de matières : bois, verre, velours, soie, fourrure et dentelle … une profusion traitée avec équilibre et raffinement. Ce qui paraîtrait surchargé ailleurs devient ici enchanteur grâce au mariage du talent, de la sophistication et de la rigueur. Il en résulte une demeure originale où tout est le fruit d'une recherche permanente du plaisir et de l'harmonie. « Une maison doit être émouvante », déclare Alan Faena qui réinvente le classicisme bourgeois d'une manière surprenante.

PREVIOUS DOUBLE PAGE:
The kitchen is a Philippe Starck design. The rough, custom-made table combines naturally with the French-style antique chairs and Murano glass chandeliers.

ABOVE LEFT:
Living room: an artwork by Andy Warhol can be seen reflected in the mirror glass doors.

BELOW LEFT:
The surprisingly happy result of a combination of styles: woven throws from the north of Argentina, the latest generation television screen framed like a painting.

RIGHT PAGE ABOVE:
The bedroom is decorated in a sophisticated, opulent manner, echoing the statement style of the rest of the house.

RIGHT PAGE BELOW:
The bathroom, also designed by Philippe Starck, with its sensual materials and Murano mirror.

VORIGE DOPPELSEITE:
Die Küche ist ein Entwurf von Philippe Starck. Der maßgefertigte Tisch aus Hartholz bildet ein harmonisches Ensemble mit den antiken Stühlen im französischen Stil und den Lüstern aus Murano-Glas.

LINKS OBEN:
Im Salon reflektieren die Spiegeltüren ein Werk von Andy Warhol.

LINKS UNTEN:
Eine glückliche Stilkombination: neben den landestypischen Decken aus Nordargentinien ein Fernseher der letzten Generation, der wie ein Gemälde gerahmt ist.

RECHTE SEITE OBEN:
Die verfeinerte, pompöse Einrichtung dieses Schlafzimmers wiederholt den kraftvollen Stil des restlichen Hauses.

RECHTE SEITE UNTEN:
Das ebenfalls von Philippe Starck entworfene Bad mit seinen sinnlichen Materialien und seinem Spiegel aus Murano-Glas.

DOUBLE PAGE PRÉCÉDENTE :
La cuisine, conçue par Philippe Starck. Une table en bois rugueux, réalisée sur mesure, des chaises anciennes de style français et des lustres en cristal de Murano.

À GAUCHE, EN HAUT :
Dans les portes en miroir du salon, on aperçoit le reflet d'une toile d'Andy Warhol.

À GAUCHE, EN BAS :
Un mariage de styles surprenant et heureux : des plaids traditionnels du nord de l'Argentine, un téléviseur high-tech encadré tel un tableau.

PAGE DE DROITE, EN HAUT :
La chambre, sophistiquée et extravagante, dans le même style frappant que le reste de la maison.

PAGE DE DROITE, EN BAS :
La salle de bains, également conçue par Philippe Starck, avec ses matériaux sensuels et son miroir de Murano.

102

ALAN FAENA / PUERTO MADERO, BUENOS AIRES

LEFT PAGE:
Alan Faena's bedroom: relief ceiling panels from an old church are reflected in the mirror.

RIGHT PAGE:
Glass plays an important role in Faena's home – a Murano glass chandelier and red crystal teardrop lamps brought back from a trip to Andalusia.

LINKE SEITE:
Im Zimmer Alans reflektiert der Spiegel die reliefierten Kassetten an der Decke aus einer alten Kirche.

RECHTE SEITE:
Neben seinen Lüstern aus Murano-Glas spielt auch Kristall in diesem Haus eine große Rolle. Die roten Kristallleuchten hat Alan auf einer Reise nach Andalusien erstanden.

PAGE DE GAUCHE :
Dans la chambre d'Alan Faena, le miroir reflète le plafond en panneaux sculptés provenant d'une vieille église.

PAGE DE DROITE :
Le verre occupe une place de premier plan dans la maison, entre les lustres de Murano et, ici, des photophores en cristal rouge garnis de pampilles achetés par Alan Faena en Andalousie.

104

ALAN FAENA / PUERTO MADERO, BUENOS AIRES

Laura Orcoyen &
Pablo Sanchez Elía

BAJO BELGRANO, BUENOS AIRES

In Argentina the name Laura Orcoyen – creator of the "Laura O." brand – is synonymous with avant-garde design. Her husband, Pablo Sanchez Elía, is one of Argentina's most prominent architects. Their home, designed by Pablo and furnished with pieces designed by Laura, is an exercise in supreme rigour. What is clear as one moves through these spaces is that despite the cleanness of vision, any sense of coldness has been kept at bay. The walls are like an enveloping skin dominated by the uniformity of the material, which is coloured, powdered marble. Each element is in harmony with the rest, none obviously dominating another; the superb quality of the design and execution creates just the right balance, expressing the demands of modernity and the art of fine craftsmanship. Pablo acknowledges the influence on his work of Vitruvius, Piero della Francesca, as well as Andrea Palladio. He produces a contemporary architecture where fine quality materials are of fundamental importance. The result is a home where this creative couple have given expression to a lifestyle of simplicity with great coherence.

LEFT PAGE:

The Zen-like feeling of the house, rising like a temple, seen from the entrance.

RIGHT:

The living room and swimming pool are linked by a veranda with a large floor-to-ceiling window. In summer this remains permanently open, bringing the "outside inside."

LINKE SEITE:

Das Haus wirkt wie ein emporstrebender Tempel, es strahlt Zen-Atmosphäre aus – hier vom Eingang aus gesehen.

RECHTS:

Wohnzimmer und Swimmingpool sind durch eine Veranda mit einem großen, vom Boden bis zur Decke reichenden Fenster verbunden. Im Sommer steht es ständig offen.

PAGE DE GAUCHE :

L'attitude zen de la maison, tel un temple tout en hauteur, vue depuis l'entrée.

À DROITE :

Une galerie qui relie le séjour et la piscine est percée d'une grande fenêtre qui va du sol au plafond. L'été, elle est toujours ouverte, conformément au concept de « l'extérieur à l'intérieur ».

107

In Argentinien gilt Laura Orcoyen, die Schöpferin der Marke Laura O., als Synonym für avantgardistisches Design und Pablo Sanchez Elía als einer der namhaftesten Architekten. Ihr Haus, von Pablo gebaut und mit den Entwürfen von Laura ausgestattet, übt sich in Strenge. Doch bald wird dem Betrachter klar, dass ungeachtet des Konzepts visueller Klarheit jegliche Kühle fehlt. Die einheitlich gestalteten Wände, die alle mit einem Putz aus feinem Marmorstaub überzogen sind, strahlen Wärme und Geborgenheit aus. Jedes Element harmoniert mit dem Rest, ohne sich vorzudrängen, und das hochwertige Design und die Ausführung, in denen moderne Ansprüche und handwerkliche Qualität zum Ausdruck kommen, haben das richtige Maß. Pablo nennt als Einfluss auf seine Arbeit Vitruv, Piero della Francesca und Andrea Palladio. Er kreiert eine zeitgenössische Architektur mit Charakter, bei der edlen Materialien eine fundamentale Bedeutung zukommt. Dieses kreative Paar hat sich mit großer Konsequenz einem schlichten und klaren Lebensstil verschrieben.

En Argentine, le nom de Laura Orcoyen, créatrice de la marque « Laura O. », est synonyme de design avant-gardiste, et celui de Pablo Sanchez Elía, d'architecte de renom. Leur maison, réalisée par Pablo et aménagée en grande partie avec les créations de Laura, est un exercice de rigueur suprême. Cependant, leur recherche de pureté visuelle est aux antipodes de la froideur. L'effet d'ensemble est celui d'un cocon où tous les espaces sont unis par l'uniformité de la matière, à savoir la poudre de marbre teintée. Chaque élément s'harmonise avec les autres sans qu'aucun ne se détache. La grande qualité du design et de l'architecture atteint un juste milieu, exprimant des exigences de modernité et de logique artisanale. Pablo reconnaît l'influence sur son travail des maîtres comme Vitruvio, Piero della Francesca et d'Andrea Palladio. Son œuvre reflète l'importance qu'il attache à la noblesse des matières et de la couleur. Ce couple de créatifs a, avec une grande cohérence, fait de la sobriété un art de vivre.

ABOVE LEFT:
*Interior designer Laura
Orcoyen with her husband
Pablo Sanchez Elía pho-
tographed on the staircase
in their house. The couple
have known each other
since they were very
young.*

BELOW LEFT:
*The interplay of verticals
and horizontals and the
different levels add to the
sensation of light, dark
and texture.*

RIGHT PAGE ABOVE:
*Dining room: a large table
seating twelve and old
family chairs that have
been reupholstered.*

RIGHT PAGE BELOW:
*In the living room, as every-
where in this house, the
pieces have been carefully
chosen. The table is made
of carob wood from the
north of Argentina and was
designed by Ricardo Paz,
an Argentinian designer
who works with Laura
Orcoyen.*

LINKS OBEN:
*Die Designerin Laura
Orcoyen und ihr Ehemann
Pablo Sanchez Elía, die sich
seit frühester Jugend ken-
nen, auf der Treppe ihres
Hauses.*

LINKS UNTEN:
*Das Spiel der Vertikalen
und Horizontalen sowie
die Höhenunterschiede ver-
stärken die Wahrnehmung
von Licht, Schatten und
Texturen.*

RECHTE SEITE OBEN:
*Im Speisezimmer bietet ein
großer Tisch mit antiken,
neu bezogenen Stühlen
aus Familienbesitz Platz für
zwölf Personen.*

RECHTE SEITE UNTEN:
*Wie alle Möbel im Haus
sind auch die des Salons
gut gewählt. Der Tisch
aus dem Holz des Johan-
nisbrotbaums aus dem
Norden des Landes ist ein
Werk von Ricardo Paz,
einem argentinischen
Designer der mit Laura
zusammenarbeitet.*

À GAUCHE, EN HAUT :
*La designer Laura Orcoyen
et son mari Pablo Sanchez
Elía se sont connus très
jeunes.*

À GAUCHE, EN BAS :
*Le jeu des lignes verticales
et horizontales, ainsi que
les différentes hauteurs
sous plafond, renforcent
les effets de lumière,
d'ombres et de textures.*

PAGE DE DROITE, EN HAUT :
*Dans la salle à manger, une
grande table de douze places et des vielles chaises
de famille retapissées.*

PAGE DE DROITE, EN BAS :
*Comme dans toute la mai-
son, chaque meuble du
salon a été soigneusement
choisi. La table basse en
caroubier, un bois que l'on
utilise beaucoup dans le
nord du pays, est de
Ricardo Paz, un designer
argentin qui travaille avec
Laura Orcoyen.*

ABOVE LEFT:
The inner staircase has
been given a sculptural
treatment. The walls have
a chromatic quality and
there is a clever use of
light. Below the stairs is a
sculpture by Ricardo Paz.

BELOW LEFT:
A lack of ostentation and
the same simple mono-
chrome colouring pervade
the bathroom, with the
simple counterpoint of a
ledge of family photo-
graphs.

RIGHT PAGE ABOVE:
Two mirrors symmetrically
arranged on each side
of the chimney breast.
White sofas and lamps
by Laura O.

RIGHT PAGE BELOW:
In the bedroom, the
furniture continues in the
same spirit of traditional
design reinvented by
Laura Orcoyen and Ricardo
Paz and made from region-
al woods from the north
of Argentina.

LINKS OBEN:
Durch eine intelligente
Lichtregie und die chroma-
tische Farbabstimmung
der Wände wird die Treppe
zur Skulptur. Unter der
Treppe ein Kunstwerk von
Ricardo Paz.

LINKS UNTEN:
Hier ist nichts Prunkvolles
zu sehen – sogar im
schlichten Badezimmer
gibt es nur aufeinander ab-
gestimmte Farben und als
Kontrapunkt ein Sims mit
Familienfotos.

RECHTE SEITE OBEN:
Zwei symmetrisch zu
beiden Seiten des Kamins
angebrachte Spiegel.
Weiße Sofas und Lampen
der Marke Laura O.

RECHTE SEITE UNTEN:
In diesem Schlafzimmer
finden sich erneut die
landestypisch inspirierten
Möbel, die Laura und
Ricardo Paz entworfen
und mit Hölzern aus dem
Norden Argentiniens reali-
siert haben.

À GAUCHE, EN HAUT :
L'escalier intérieur, traité
comme une sculpture.
Chromatisme des murs
et subtile mise en valeur
de la lumière. Sous les
marches, une sculpture
de Ricardo Paz.

À GAUCHE, EN BAS :
Aucune ostentation dans
la salle de bains, où la monochromie est toujours de
rigueur. Sur la corniche,
une série de photos de
famille.

PAGE DE DROITE, EN HAUT :
Deux miroirs placés symé-
triquement de chaque côté
de la cheminée. Canapés
blancs et lampadaires
de Laura O.

PAGE DE DROITE, EN BAS :
Dans la chambre, on re-
trouve des pièces créées
par Laura Orcoyen et
Ricardo Paz s'inspirant du
mobilier artisanal et réalisées dans des bois du nord
de l'Argentine.

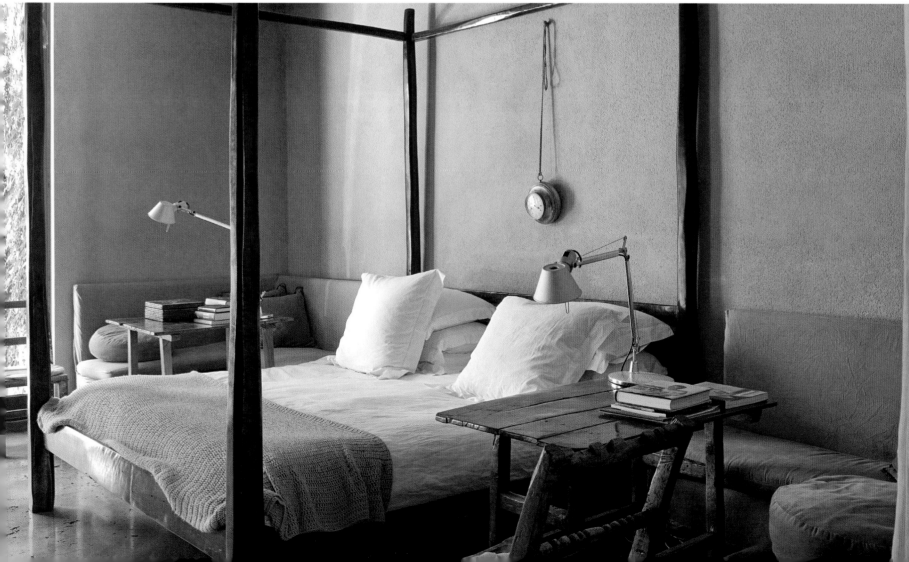

VILLA OCAMPO

VICTORIA OCAMPO

SAN ISIDRO

Victoria Ocampo was one of Argentina's most famous women, both inside and outside the country. She devoted her enormous fortune to creating the magazine "Sur", first published in 1931 – a cultural endeavour that opened a window on to the world for 20th-century Argentine literature and thinking. Her house, now owned by UNESCO, was built by her father in 1891 and in 1940 became the writer's permanent home. It contains an important collection of books, works of art, furniture and personal items that reflect Ocampo's taste for fine, simple objects associated with the domestic, creole tradition in which a love of fine materials and large spaces prevails. Villa Ocampo is one Argentina's most interesting houses because of the many celebrated guests who passed through it at Ocampo's invitation. They included Rabindranath Tagore, Roger Caillois, André Malraux, Albert Camus, Federico García Lorca and Pierre Drieu La Rochelle. As a meeting place for writers such as Jorge Luis Borges and Adolfo Bioy Casares, it is also steeped in the literary history of Argentina.

LEFT PAGE:

With its English and French influences, Villa Ocampo is one of the most interesting houses in Argentina in terms of its history and architecture.

LEFT:

The house is situated against the backdrop of the River Plate and surrounded by a vast garden. In this majestic and impressive setting, Ocampo maintained a stately but unstuffy atmosphere.

LINKE SEITE:

Die Villa Ocampo mit ihren englischen und französischen Stilelementen stellt aufgrund ihrer Geschichte und Architektur einen der interessantesten Wohnsitze Argentiniens dar.

LINKS:

Das von einem riesigen Garten umgebene Haus liegt am Río de la Plata. In diesem eindrucksvollen und majestätischen Rahmen wusste Victoria eine herrschaftliche und doch zugleich unprätentiöse Atmosphäre zu schaffen.

PAGE DE GAUCHE :

D'influence anglaise et française, la villa Ocampo est l'une des demeures les plus intéressantes d'Argentine par son histoire et son architecture.

À GAUCHE :

La villa, entourée d'un immense jardin, se dresse au bord du Río de la Plata. Victoria Ocampo a conservé son climat seigneurial mais sans emphase.

Victoria Ocampo war eine weit über Argentinien hinaus berühmte Frau. Sie steckte ihr ansehnliches Vermögen in die Kulturzeitschrift „Sur" und einen Verlag, den sie 1931 gründete und der der argentinischen Literatur des 20. Jahrhunderts ein Fenster zur Welt öffnete. Ihre Villa, heute Eigentum der UNESCO, wurde 1891 von ihrem Vater errichtet und ab 1940 ständiger Wohnsitz der Schriftstellerin. Sie besaß eine imposante Sammlung von Büchern, Kunstwerken, Möbeln und persönlichen Gegenständen, in denen sich ihre Vorliebe für schlichte Dinge aus der kreolischen Familientradition zeigt und in der edle Materialien und Weiträumigkeit dominieren. Victoria führte ein großes Haus, in dem sie Gäste wie Rabindranath Tagore, Roger Caillois, André Malraux, Albert Camus, Federico García Lorca oder Pierre Drieu La Rochelle empfing – daher gehört diese Villa zu den interessantesten Wohnsitzen Argentiniens. Zugleich ist es auch das erinnerungsträchtigste Haus der argentinischen Literatur, war es doch Treffpunkt für Schriftsteller wie Jorge Luis Borges und Adolfo Bioy Casares.

Victoria Ocampo fut l'une des Argentines les plus célèbres dans et hors de son pays. Elle consacra son immense fortune à sa revue culturelle « Sur », fondée en 1931, qui fut, pour le monde, une fenêtre sur les lettres et la pensée argentines du 20e siècle. Sa demeure, qui appartient désormais à l'UNESCO, fut construite par son père en 1891. Elle devint la résidence permanente de l'écrivain à partir de 1940. Elle abrite une importante collection d'ouvrages, d'œuvres d'art, de meubles et d'objets personnels qui illustrent le goût d'Ocampo pour les choses simples et nobles, reflet d'une tradition familiale de bonne souche argentine. Ses murs ont vu défiler de nombreux grands intellectuels étrangers invités par la maîtresse de maison : Rabindranath Tagore, Roger Caillois, André Malraux, Albert Camus, Federico García Lorca, Pierre Drieu La Rochelle, entre autres. Le gratin des écrivains argentins s'y réunissait, dont Jorge Luis Borges et Adolfo Bioy Casares, écrivant un des chapitres les plus remarquables de littérature nationale.

ABOVE LEFT:
Photo portrait of Victoria Ocampo made in Paris by Man Ray. She is wearing Chanel and was one of the fashion house's first clients.

BELOW LEFT:
In keeping with the style of the house, the staircase with its original wooden banister is simple yet elegant.

RIGHT PAGE ABOVE:
A rug based on a design by Picasso hangs as a tapestry over the fireplace. Someone once stubbed out a cigarette on it, which is why it is now on the wall. A pair of white armchairs stand side by side with others in Louis XV style and some early 20th-century Austrian chairs.

RIGHT PAGE BELOW:
The dining room reflects Ocampo's taste for simplicity. The chairs have straw seats and backs, like those she used to decorate her Paris apartment in the 1930s. The painting is by the famous Argentinian artist Prilidiano Pueyrredón.

LINKS OBEN:
Porträt von Victoria Ocampo, das Man Ray von ihr in Paris machte. Sie trägt Mode von Coco Chanel, zu deren ersten Kundinnen sie gehörte.

LINKS UNTEN:
Im Einklang mit dem Stil des Hauses ist die Treppe mit dem originalen Holzgeländer schlicht und elegant zugleich.

RECHTE SEITE OBEN:
Der Teppich nach einem Entwurf von Picasso wurde als Wandteppich über den Kamin verbannt, nachdem jemand ein Zigarillo auf ihm ausgedrückt hatte. Am Kamin zwei Sessel im Stil Louis XV. neben zwei weißen Klubsesseln und österreichischen Stühlen vom Anfang des 20. Jahrhunderts.

RECHTE SEITE UNTEN:
Das Speisezimmer zeigt Victorias Vorliebe für schlichte Dinge. Die Stühle aus Strohgeflecht gleichen jenen, die sie in den 1930er-Jahren zur Einrichtung ihres Apartments in Paris verwendete. An der Wand ein Gemälde des berühmten argentinischen Malers Prilidiano Pueyrredón.

À GAUCHE, EN HAUT :
Portrait de Victoria Ocampo réalisé à Paris par Man Ray. Elle fut l'une des premières clientes de Chanel.

À GAUCHE, EN BAS :
Correspondant bien au style de la maison, l'escalier, avec sa rampe d'origine en bois, est sobre et élégant.

PAGE DE DROITE, EN HAUT :
Au-dessus de la cheminée, un tapis d'après un motif de Picasso. Il fut accroché au mur après que quelqu'un ait écrasé sa cigarette dessus. Les fauteuils blancs et les sièges de style Louis XV cohabitent avec des chaises autrichiennes du début du 20e siècle.

PAGE DE DROITE, EN BAS :
La salle à manger illustre le goût de Victoria pour les choses simples. Elle possédait le même type de chaises cannées dans son appartement parisien dans les années 1930. Tableau du célèbre peintre argentin Prilidiano Pueyrredón.

LEFT PAGE:
The portrait of Virginia Woolf is by photographer Gisèle Freund and was commissioned by Ocampo. The second from left shows Rabindranath Tagore at Villa Ocampo and right-most the portrait of Nehru. Hanging above is a portrait of Victoria Ocampo herself by the French painter Dagnan-Bouveret.

RIGHT PAGE:
Another view of the living room, which Ocampo referred to as "the corner room." On the table is a collection of photographs of celebrities of the period who became her friends.

LINKE SEITE:
Auf der Ablage links ein Porträt von Virginia Woolf, das im Auftrag Victorias von der Fotografin Gisèle Freund aufgenommen wurde. Auf einer anderen Fotografie ist Tagore während seines Besuches in der Villa Ocampo zu sehen. Rechts davon ein Porträt Nehrus. An der Wand ein von dem französischen Maler Dagnan-Bouveret geschaffenes Porträt von Victoria Ocampo.

116

RECHTE SEITE:
Eine andere Ansicht des Salons, den Victoria „das Eckzimmer" nannte. Auf dem Tisch Fotografien von Berühmtheiten, die zu ihrem Freundeskreis zählten.

PAGE DE GAUCHE :
Une photo de Tagore à la villa Ocampo et un portrait de Virginia Woolf réalisé par Gisèle Freund à la de-mande de Victoria Ocampo. À droite un portrait de Nehru. Au mur, un portrait de la maîtresse de maison par le peintre français Dagnan-Bouveret.

PAGE DE DROITE :
Une autre vue du salon que Victoria Ocampo appe-lait « la pièce du coin ». Sur la table, un bataillon de photographies de célébrités amies de la maîtresse de maison.

Casa San Isidro

SAN ISIDRO

A large green space to the north of Buenos Aires, a photographer, a fashion designer and Argentina's Production of Contemporary Architecture studio (PAC) are the foundations on which this timeless, two-storey dwelling was constructed. "The first thought we had was that it should be possible to see right through the house and that it should be at one with its surroundings," explains architect Martín Olabarrieta. "From that came the decision not to interrupt the glazing with frames and bars," he goes on. Achieving privacy in each environment without losing the sense of continuity was another of the challenges that the architects set themselves, achieving this by varying the materials – glass, wood, plant screens and stone walls – but also by using subtle dividers like the floating staircase, the metal kitchen furniture and simple variations in floor level. "This work may be futuristic, modern or classical, but the materials and the particular way they are used make it Argentinian through and through," Olabarrieta concludes.

LEFT PAGE:
An outdoor fireplace set in a dry stone wall inside a gabion of thick metal mesh. Behind, against the wall, is a grill for roasting meat.

LEFT:
Rear view of the house showing part of the floating volume of the first floor. On the patio is a zoomorphic seat carved by the Argentinian artist Ricardo Marcenaro.

LINKE SEITE:
In Trockenbauweise errichtete Steinmauer mit Maschendraht und Feuerstelle. Dahinter befindet sich ein an der Mauer befestigter Grillrost für asados (gegrilltes Fleisch).

LINKS:
Rückansicht des Hauses: der „schwebende" Baukörper des Obergeschosses. Im Patio ein von dem argentinischen Künstler Ricardo Marcenaro skulptierter zoomorpher Sitz.

PAGE DE GAUCHE :
Un foyer extérieur dans le mur en pierres sèches et maille métallique. Derrière se cache un gril pour les asados (grillades).

À GAUCHE :
L'arrière de la maison, avec une partie de l'étage en saillie. Sur la terrasse, un siège zoomorphe de l'artiste argentin Ricardo Marcenaro.

Auf einer großen Grünfläche im Norden von Buenos Aires errichteten ein Fotograf, eine Modedesignerin und das argentinische Architekturbüro PAC (Producción de Arquitectura Contemporánea) ein zeitloses zweigeschossiges Haus. „Wir wollten ein Haus bauen, das visuelle Durchblicke erlaubt und eine Einheit mit der Umgebung bildet", erzählt der Architekt Martín Olabarrieta. „Daher trafen wir die Entscheidung, die Verglasungen nicht zu unterbrechen." Eine weitere Herausforderung, der sich die Architekten stellten, lag darin, jedem Raum Intimität zu verleihen, ohne das Gefühl der Kontinuität zu verlieren. Sie lösten diese Aufgabe durch Verwendung unterschiedlicher Materialien (Glas, Holz, durch Pflanzen betonte Wände oder Steinmauerwerk) und mit subtilen Details wie einer schwebenden Treppe, einem großen Küchenmöbel aus Stahl oder einfach durch Höhenunterschiede. „Dieses Haus könnte futuristisch, modern oder klassisch genannt werden", bekräftigt Martín, „aber seine Materialien und deren besonderer Einsatz kennzeichnen es als argentinisch."

Un grand espace vert au nord de Buenos Aires, un photographe, une styliste de mode, le cabinet d'architecture PAC (Producción de Arquitectura Contemporánea), tels furent les bases de cette structure atemporelle d'un étage. « Nous sommes partis de l'idée qu'on puisse voir à travers toute la maison et que celle-ci se fonde dans son environnement », explique l'architecte Martín Olabarrieta. « À partir de là, la décision d'éviter la menuiserie qui interrompait les vitres s'est imposée d'elle-même ». L'autre défi consistait à conférer de l'intimité à chaque pièce sans rompre l'impression de continuité. La solution : des changements de matières – vitre, bois, murs végétaux ou en pierre – ainsi que des divisions subtiles tels qu'un escalier flottant, le meuble en métal de la cuisine ou de simples différences de niveau. « Ce pourrait être une œuvre futuriste, moderne, classique mais, par ses matériaux et l'usage qu'il en est fait, elle est par essence argentine », conclut Olabarrieta.

ABOVE LEFT:
Exercise area and decking terrace with central stone fire pit, located on the floating block. Wood and glass continue to be the dominant materials.

BELOW LEFT:
The kitchen – a rectangle of glass and stone broken only by the steel island, designed to create a single, visual block.

RIGHT PAGE ABOVE:
Front of the house with the living area concealed behind a small mound, and the floating volume of the first floor where the bedrooms are located.

RIGHT PAGE BELOW:
The pool, breaking the horizontal line of the house but built in the same materials as the rest. At the far end is a waterfall wall which is also the wall of the changing room.

LINKS OBEN:
Im „schwebenden" Baukörper sind der Fitnessraum und die Terrasse aus Holz mit dem für Lagerfeuer präparierten Zentrum aus Stein untergebracht. Holz und Glas sind weiterhin die vorherrschenden Baustoffe.

LINKS UNTEN:
Die Küche, ein Rechteck aus Glas und Stein, wird nur durch eine Insel aus Stahl unterbrochen, die einen einzigen visuellen Block bildet.

RECHTE SEITE OBEN:
Vorderseite des Hauses mit dem Wohnbereich hinter einem Dickicht und die „schwebenden" seitlichen Auskragungen des Obergeschosses, in dem sich Schlafzimmer befinden.

RECHTE SEITE UNTEN:
Der Swimmingpool, bei dem dieselben Materialien wie im übrigen Komplex verwendet wurden, setzt die horizontale Ausrichtung des Hauses fort. Im Hintergrund eine Mauer mit einer Kaskade, die zugleich die Wand des Umkleideraums bildet.

À GAUCHE, EN HAUT :
Dans le bloc en saillie, le coin gym et une terrasse encastrée d'un petit salon tapissé de gravier où l'on peut faire du feu. Ici aussi, le bois et le verre prédominent.

À GAUCHE, EN BAS :
La cuisine, rectangle de vitre et de pierre interrompu par l'îlot, est conçue comme un seul bloc visuel.

PAGE DE DROITE, EN HAUT :
La façade avant est nichée derrière une colline qui protège le séjour. Le premier étage en saillie abrite les chambres à coucher.

PAGE DE DROITE, EN BAS :
La piscine prolonge la ligne horizontale de la maison et recourt aux mêmes matériaux. Au fond, un mur avec cascade derrière lequel se cache un vestiaire.

The kitchen wall consists of
three successive planes:
dry stone walling, glass and
concrete.

Die Küchenwand besteht
aus drei aufeinanderfolgen-
den Flächen: einer in Trockenbauweise errichteten
Mauer, einer Glaswand und
einer Betonwand.

Le mur de la cuisine est
composé de trois plans
successifs : pierres sèches,
vitre et mur en béton.

122

ABOVE LEFT:
Floating concrete staircase dressed in lapacho hardwood. The wood sculptures are by Ricardo Marcenaro.

BELOW LEFT:
The master bedroom is a large box lined with lapacho wood, interrupted only by the windows.

RIGHT PAGE:
Living room with solid plate-glass wall facing the front. Table and stools carved in eucalyptus wood from a tree that had to be felled to provide the best site for the house; most of the furniture was made from this tree.

LINKS OBEN:
Schwebende Betontreppe, die mit Lapacho-Holz verkleidet ist. Die Holzskulpturen sind von Ricardo Marcenaro.

LINKS UNTEN:
Das Schlafzimmer der Hausbesitzer ist mit Lapacho-Holz ausgekleidet.

RECHTE SEITE:
Das Wohnzimmer mit seiner durchgehenden Vorderfront aus Glas. Tisch und Hocker sind aus dem Holz eines Eukalyptusbaums geschnitzt, der einst auf dem Grundstück stand und bei Baubeginn gefällt werden musste. Ein Großteil der Möbel wurde aus dem Holz dieses Baums gefertigt.

À GAUCHE, EN HAUT :
Escalier flottant en béton revêtu d'un placage en lapacho. *Des sculptures en bois de Ricardo Marcenaro.*

À GAUCHE, EN BAS :
Les murs de la chambre principale sont revêtus d'un placage en lapacho.

PAGE DE DROITE :
Le séjour avec un grand mur de verre donnant sur l'extérieur. La table et les bancs ont été sculptés dans un eucalyptus qu'il a fallu abattre pour construire la maison et qui a fourni la matière première de la plupart des meubles.

124

CASA SAN ISIDRO / SAN ISIDRO

LA MARTINA

CAÑUELAS

Just 50 kilometres outside the city of Buenos Aires it is open countryside. A fine polo field borders the front of this imposing two-storey house. Here we discover pure volumes, flat roofs, textured rendering, openings that extend up to the roof, fine materials and paradoxically intimate environments within a piece of monumental architecture. The living spaces are an arrival point and meeting place where once again the interplay of texture, form, volume and colour brings a sense of tranquillity, repose and quality of life. For architect Pablo Sanchez Elía and interior designer Laura Orcoyen, the underlying premise appears to be experiencing improved quality of life by rediscovering the luxury of space. "This house is all about the natural elements; it is in touch with fire, water and air," explains Pablo. "The landscape comes into the house and into all the transit areas, and the green of the surroundings is a constant presence." Inside, solid, homely furniture and the *neocriollo* style – a fusion of European furniture and Argentinian materials – come into their own.

PREVIOUS DOUBLE PAGE:
Simplicity of volume, classicism and timelessness in this two-storey house rising up against a verdant backdrop.

LEFT PAGE:
Blocks of box hedging frame this contemporary "little château" and a low stone border surrounds the building.

RIGHT:
View from the central veranda on one of the climber-covered pergolas that create a fluid transition between exterior and interior.

VORIGE DOPPELSEITE:
Schlichtheit der Volumen, Klassizismus und Zeitlosigkeit prägen dieses zweigeschossige Haus, das sich inmitten einer Grünfläche erhebt.

LINKE SEITE:
Gruppen von Buchsbäumen um das zeitgenössische „petit château" und die steinerne Einfassung des Hauses.

RECHTS:
Blick von der zentralen Terrasse auf eine der Pergolen mit ihren üppig rankenden Schlingpflanzen, die einen fließenden Übergang zwischen innen und außen schaffen.

DOUBLE PAGE PRÉCÉDENTE :
Simplicité des volumes, classicisme et atemporalité dans un cadre de verdure.

PAGE DE GAUCHE :
Des massifs de buis et une ligne en pierre encadrent le « petit château » contemporain.

À DROITE :
Vue depuis la galerie centrale, une des pergolas envahies de plantes grimpantes qui créent une transition fluide entre l'extérieur et l'intérieur.

Nur 50 Kilometer von Buenos Aires entfernt erstreckt sich schon die weite Landschaft der Pampa. Der Front des imposanten zweigeschossigen Hauses ist ein Polo-Spielfeld vorgelagert. Das Gebäude selbst zeichnet sich aus durch klare Volumen, flache Dächer, groben Putz, raumhohe Öffnungen, edle Materialien und für diese monumentale Architektur erstaunlich intime Räume. Ort der Begegnung sind die Eingangsbereiche und Aufenthaltsräume, in denen das Spiel zwischen Form, Volumen, Textur und Farbe Ruhe ausstrahlt und so für Entspannung und Lebensqualität sorgt. Für den Architekten Pablo Sanchez Elía und die Designerin Laura Orcoyen scheinen großzügige Räumlichkeiten eine Voraussetzung für gutes Lebens zu sein. „Dieses Haus hat mit den Elementen der Natur zu tun, es steht in Verbindung mit dem Feuer, dem Wasser und der Luft", erklärt Pablo. „Die Landschaft und das Grün der Umgebung sind hier überall präsent." Im Inneren tragen die soliden Möbel der Familie und der *estilo neocriollo* (der neukreolische Stil) durch die Verschmelzung von europäischen Möbeln und argentinischen Materialien das ihre dazu bei.

À une cinquantaine de kilomètres de Buenos Aires, là où la campagne s'étend à perte de vue, cette imposante demeure de deux étages se dresse devant un terrain de polo. Elle se distingue par ses volumes purs, des toits plats, des enduits texturés, des ouvertures qui s'étirent jusqu'au plafond, des matériaux nobles et des pièces paradoxalement intimes en dépit d'une structure monumentale. La lumière et l'architecture s'unissent pour procurer tout un éventail de sensations de plaisir. Dans les séjours, aménagés avec de robustes meubles de famille et le style *neocriollo*, synthèse d'une esthétique européenne et de matières argentines, le jeu des textures, des formes, des volumes et des couleurs est au service de la tranquillité, du repos et du bien-être. Pour l'architecte Pablo Sanchez Elía et la designer Laura Orcoyen, mieux vivre et jouir du luxe de l'espace est une priorité. « Cette maison est liée à tous les éléments de la nature », expliquent-ils. « Elle est en relation avec le feu, l'eau et l'air. Le paysage pénètre à l'intérieur et circule dans les pièces ; la verdure est omniprésente. »

LEFT PAGE:
Table and bench made from lapacho *wood from the north of Argentina and designed by Laura Orcoyen.*

ABOVE RIGHT:
Entrance porch in the traditional style on the elevation facing the wood and creating a link between interior and exterior. The lapacho *wood doorway extends upwards almost to the roof.*

BELOW RIGHT:
One of the porticoed verandas which extend along the front of the house, softening the severity of the volumes and creating a transitional space between interior and exterior.

LINKE SEITE:
Tisch und Bänke aus Lapacho-Holz aus dem Norden Argentiniens, entworfen von Laura Orcoyen.

RECHTS OBEN:
Der überdachte Vorraum des Eingangs erinnert an die traditionelle Bauweise und schafft eine Verbindung zwischen innen und außen. Die Tür aus Lapacho-Holz reicht fast bis zum Dach.

RECHTS UNTEN:
Eine der überdachten Terrassen, deren Säulen sich über die ganze Vorderseite hinweg wiederholen; sie lassen die strengen Volumen weicher erscheinen und schaffen einen Übergang zwischen innen und außen. Im Vordergrund der Swimmingpool.

PAGE DE GAUCHE :
Une table et des bancs en lapacho, un bois du nord de l'Argentine, dessinés par Laura Orcoyen.

À DROITE, EN HAUT :
La façade, qui donne sur une forêt, est mise en valeur par un porche à l'antique. La porte d'entrée en lapacho grimpe presque jusqu'au toit.

À DROITE, EN BAS :
Le portique, qui longe toute la façade avant, adoucit les volumes et crée une transition entre l'extérieur et l'intérieur. Devant, la piscine.

LA MARTINA / CAÑUELAS

ABOVE LEFT:
Swimming pool of travertine stone from the Andes.

BELOW LEFT:
Swimming pool with slight variation in the level of the land, defining the boundaries of the house by enclosing it.

RIGHT PAGE:
The veranda with linen panels to provide protection from the sun and a suite of lapacho-wood furniture. On the table a wooden trough from the north of Argentina.

LINKS OBEN:
Der Swimmingpool aus Travertin, der aus den Anden stammt.

LINKS UNTEN:
Der Swimmingpool und die kleine Bodenerhöhung, die das Haus wie eine Plattform trägt und umschließt.

RECHTE SEITE:
Die überdachte Terrasse mit Leinenvorhängen als Sonnenschutz und einer Sitzgruppe aus Lapacho-Holz. Auf dem Tisch eine flache bootähnliche Schale.

À GAUCHE, EN HAUT :
La piscine, construite en travertin andin.

À GAUCHE, EN BAS :
La piscine et la petite dénivellation qui délimite le terrain autour de la maison.

PAGE DE DROITE :
La galerie, avec des rideaux en lin pour se protéger du soleil, et des meubles en lapacho. Sur la table basse, un plateau du nord de l'Argentine.

LA MARTINA / CAÑUELAS

134

ABOVE LEFT:
Kitchen: the same materials as are used in the rest of house. The aluminium stools have lapacho wood seats and the floor is made of stone.

BELOW LEFT:
One of the bedrooms on the ground floor, with a four poster bed, and lapacho-wood table, designed to be adapted for different uses.

RIGHT PAGE ABOVE:
In the living room, furniture and objects in what is known as the neocriollo style – a fusion of European furniture and Argentinian materials, with cushions in various types of Argentine leather.

RIGHT PAGE BELOW:
On the upper floor, bed with fabric backboard, a device used by the designer to conceal the absence of a wall, and fireplace in travertine stone from the Andes.

LINKS OBEN:
In der Küche sieht man dieselben Materialien wie im übrigen Haus, etwa bei den Hockern aus Lapacho und Aluminium und beim Steinbelag des Bodens.

LINKS UNTEN:
In einem der Schlafzimmer im Erdgeschoss ein Bett mit Baldachin und ein Tisch aus Lapacho-Holz.

RECHTE SEITE OBEN:
Im Wohnzimmer ein Beispiel für den estilo neocriollo (neukreolischen Stil), eine Verschmelzung von europäischen Möbeln und argentinischen Materialien, wie die Sitzkissen aus verschiedenen argentinischen Lederarten auf dem Sofa.

RECHTE SEITE UNTEN:
Im Obergeschoss das Bett mit einem Vorhang hinter dem Kopfteil, ein Hilfsmittel der Designerin, um zu verbergen, dass hier eine Mauer fehlt, sowie ein Kamin aus Travertin, der aus den Anden stammt.

À GAUCHE, EN HAUT :
Dans la cuisine, on retrouve les mêmes matériaux. Le comptoir et les chaises sont en aluminium et lapacho. Le sol est en pierre.

À GAUCHE, EN BAS :
Dans une des chambres du rez-de-chaussée, un lit à baldaquin et une table en lapacho.

PAGE DE DROITE, EN HAUT :
Dans le séjour, ce qu'on appelle le neocriollo : une fusion de meubles européens et de matériaux argentins. Les coussins sont en différents types de cuir argentin.

PAGE DE DROITE, EN BAS :
Dans une chambre du premier étage, un rideau fait office de tête de lit afin de palier à l'absence de mur. La cheminée est en travertin andin.

LEFT PAGE:
In the bathroom, a fusion of the materials used throughout the house. The washbasins, bathtub and floor are in travertine stone from the Andes.

RIGHT PAGE:
Like a lava flow, stone covers the entire staircase linking the two floors.

LINKE SEITE:
Im Bad findet sich eine Synthese der im ganzen Haus verwendeten Materialien. Badewanne, Waschbecken und Bodenbelag sind aus Travertin.

RECHTE SEITE:
Wie Lava fließt der Steinbelag über die Treppe, die beide Geschosse verbindet.

PAGE DE GAUCHE :
Dans la salle de bains, une synthèse de toutes les matières utilisées dans le reste de la maison. Baignoire, sol et lavabo en travertin andin.

PAGE DE DROITE :
L'escalier qui relie les deux niveaux, revêtu de pierre telle une coulée de lave.

136

Paula Cahen d'Anvers & Federico Álvarez Castillo

MONTE

With a career in fashion design, an aristocratic name, two wonderful children and married to the highly successful businessman Federico Álvarez Castillo, Paula Cahen d'Anvers embodies the romantic and sophisticated feminist ideal. Following in the tradition of her grandmother and mother, she has built a country house 100 kilometres from the centre of Buenos Aires on land adjacent to her family's property. The dwelling consists of various rooms, a vast garden filled with rose-covered pergolas, an orchard and a magnificent swimming pool. The whole property was designed by Paula and in particular by her husband Federico. The building comprises different, independent yet unseparated spaces for the greater comfort of occupants and guests. The décor has been carefully thought through, down to the smallest detail, and recreates the tranquillity of the past but without abandoning modern comfort in the least. "We looked for a style that would bring new life to the traditional approach, with antique touches that would help to create the feeling that this house has been standing here for many years," the owners explain.

LEFT PAGE:
A luxuriant woodland of eucalyptus, she-oak and ombú plants protects the property.

LEFT:
The verticality of these ancient trees brings balance to this totally flat landscape.

LINKE SEITE:
Eine dicht belaubte Baumgruppe aus Eukalyptusbäumen, Kasuarinen und ombú-Pflanzen umgibt den Wohnsitz in der Pampa.

LINKS:
Die Vertikalität der 100-jährigen Bäume bildet ein harmonisches Gegengewicht zur vollkommen flachen Landschaft.

PAGE DE GAUCHE :
Un luxuriant bosquet d'eucalyptus, de casuarinas et d'ombú protège la propriété.

À GAUCHE :
La verticalité des arbres centenaires équilibre le paysage totalement horizontal.

139

Mit einer Karriere als Modedesignerin, einem aristokratischen Namen und zwei prächtigen Kindern verkörpert Paula Cahen d'Anvers, die mit dem erfolgreichen Unternehmer Federico Álvarez Castillo verheiratet ist, das Ideal romantischer feinsinniger Weiblichkeit. Mutter und Großmutter folgend hat sie sich etwa 100 Kilometer von Buenos Aires entfernt ein Haus auf dem Land neben dem Grundbesitz ihrer Familie bauen lassen. Der Wohnsitz umfasst verschiedene Nebengebäude, einen riesigen Garten mit rosenbewachsenen Pergolen sowie einen Obst- und Gemüsegarten. Der Komplex wurde von Paula und vor allem ihrem Mann Federico entworfen. Er besteht aus verschiedenen unabhängigen, aber miteinander verbundenen Baukörpern, sodass sich die Bewohner und Gäste bequem bewegen können. Die Dekoration ist bis ins Kleinste Detail durchdacht und lässt die Gemütlichkeit vergangener Tage aufkommen, ohne auf zeitgemäßen Komfort zu verzichten. „Wir suchten einen Stil, der das Traditionelle verjüngen, aber mit antiken Noten den Eindruck heraufbeschwören sollte, dass dieses Haus schon viele Jahre hier steht", erklären die Hausherren.

Avec une carrière de styliste de mode, un nom aristocratique, deux superbes enfants et un mariage avec le brillant homme d'affaires Federico Álvarez Castillo, Paula Cahen d'Anvers incarne l'idéal d'un féminisme romantique et sophistiqué. Suivant l'exemple de sa grand-mère et de sa mère, elle s'est fait construire une maison de campagne sur un terrain jouxtant le domaine familial, à cent kilomètre de la capitale. Elle compte plusieurs dépendances, un immense jardin parsemé de pergolas envahies de rosiers, un potager et une magnifique piscine. Paula et son mari ont voulu une maison qui soit pratique à vivre pour eux et leurs invités : elle est composée de plusieurs volumes indépendants mais reliés entre eux. La décoration, soignée dans ses moindres détails, vise à recréer la quiétude du passé sans renoncer en rien au confort moderne. « Nous cherchons un style qui rajeunisse la vision du traditionnel, avec des touches anciennes qui donnent l'impression que cette maison existe depuis toujours », expliquent les propriétaires.

142

PREVIOUS DOUBLE PAGE:
The infinity pool merges into the distant horizon. Its refined simplicity creates a wonderful sense of serene beauty reflected in the elegant wrought iron loungers.

ABOVE LEFT:
View of one of the parts of the house intended for occasional guests. The idea was to provide a separate retreat where the slow pace of rural life, immersed in nature, could be enjoyed.

BELOW LEFT:
The seating was designed by Federico. The double-height room provides a mezzanine area that is used as a relaxation and reading space.

RIGHT PAGE ABOVE:
Exterior view: with impeccable décor and a perfect natural setting, the house invites quiet contemplation but is also a place where friends can get together to enjoy a traditional barbecue.

RIGHT PAGE BELOW:
Living room: the fire surround is made from timber sourced from old beams; the wall above is covered in pictures and family photos. "We wanted it to be very welcoming, as we love using this space," explains Paula.

VORIGE DOPPELSEITE:
Der Infinity Pool geht in den fernen Horizont über. Seine klare und schlichte Form strahlt elegante Schönheit aus. Am Beckenrand stehen einige gepolsterte Liegen aus Schmiedeeisen.

LINKS OBEN:
Blick auf ein für Gäste bestimmtes Gebäude des Wohnkomplexes. Ziel war es, ein unabhängiges Refugium zu schaffen, um ein Leben im ländlichen Rhythmus und mit der Natur zu ermöglichen.

LINKS UNTEN:
Die Sofas wurden von Federico entworfen. Die Empore dient als Ruheraum und Leseecke.

RECHTE SEITE OBEN:
Das makellos gestaltete Haus inmitten einer vollkommenen Natur fördert die Kontemplation, wenngleich man sich hier auch mit Freunden in geselliger Runde zu asado (gegrilltem Fleisch) trifft.

RECHTE SEITE UNTEN:
Im Wohnzimmer wurde der Kamin mit dem Holz alter Balken umkleidet, während die Wand mit Bildern und Fotos der Familie bedeckt ist. „Wir wollten es gemütlich haben, da wir diesen Raum sehr gern nutzen", berichtet Paula.

DOUBLE PAGE PRÉCÉDENTE :
La piscine, au ras du sol, se fond dans le paysage plat qui s'étend à perte de vue et participe à sa beauté sereine. Autour, des chaises longues en fer forgé.

À GAUCHE, EN HAUT :
Un des bâtiments, réservé aux invités. Il constitue un refuge indépendant ou l'on peut vivre au rythme de la campagne et immergé dans la nature.

À GAUCHE, EN BAS :
Les canapés ont été dessinés par le maître de maison. La double hauteur sous plafond a permis de créer une salle de détente et de lecture en mezzanine.

PAGE DE DROITE, EN HAUT :
Un pavillon ouvert aux éléments, une décoration impeccable, une nature parfaite : l'atmosphère propice à une contemplation permanente. On s'y retrouve avec les amis pour partager de généreux barbecues.

PAGE DE DROITE, EN BAS :
Dans le salon, une cheminée dont le cadre a été réalisé avec du bois de récupération. Aux murs, des tableaux et photos de famille. « Nous l'avons voulu le plus chaleureux possible car c'est là que nous passons le plus de temps », confie la maîtresse de maison.

LEFT PAGE:
The master bedroom has an adjoining bathroom. The pictures are from Paula's grandmother's house and the chequered floor tiles are reclaimed.

RIGHT PAGE:
The same aesthetic applies in the kitchen as in the rest of the house: vintage table, lamps and flooring.

LINKE SEITE:
Das Hauptschlafzimmer hat sein eigenes Badezimmer. Die Bilder stammen aus dem Haus von Paulas Groß-mutter und die schachbrett-artig verlegten Fliesen aus Abrisshäusern.

RECHTE SEITE:
In der Küche herrscht dieselbe Ästhetik wie im übrigen Haus: Vintage-Tisch und -Lampen sowie alte Bodenfliesen.

PAGE DE GAUCHE :
La chambre principale communique avec sa salle de bains. Les tableaux venant de chez la grand-mère de Paula Cahen d'Anvers et sol en damier réalisé avec des carreaux de récupération.

144

PAGE DE DROITE :
Dans la cuisine, la même esthétique que dans le reste de la maison : tables, lampes et sols anciens.

PAULA CAHEN D'ANVERS & FEDERICO ÁLVAREZ CASTILLO / MONTE

ALICIA GOÑI

GENERAL RODRÍGUEZ

Along with her partner Florencia Pieres, Alicia Goñi is the creator of fashion and houseware boutiques known as Cat Ballou, renowned for the mould-breaking, relaxed, informal style they offer. And it is Goñi who has restyled this old house belonging to her family at the Los Fresnos polo field in Buenos Aires Province. The setting is magnificent. Amid the immensity of the *pampa* stands this unpretentious dwelling executed with one simple philosophy in mind: to respect and adapt to the environment around it. To make it seem as if the building has always been there, reclaimed materials have been used to give it a feeling of age – old beams, doors and windows lend it the stamp of authenticity. But the dominant mood comes from the colours and textures. "I love getting hold of old furniture and transforming it." Though it may appear simple on the outside, inside this house is a wealth of elegance and comfort as Goñi displays many of her qualities as an interior designer and painter.

LEFT PAGE:

Movable candle holders made by Goñi using empty yoghurt jars held by wires.

RIGHT:

The walls are painted pale yellow and almond green, Goñi's favourite colours which, as she explains, are "tones that improve with age." The iron bed frame is an old piece of family furniture.

LINKE SEITE:

Die Kerzenlichter fertigte Alicia aus Joghurtgläsern, die sie mit Draht am Baum befestigte.

RECHTS:

Die Wände wurden gelb und mandelgrün gestrichen, die Lieblingsfarben Alicias, die versichert: „Diese Farbtöne werden mit der Zeit immer schöner." Das eiserne Bett stammt aus Familienbesitz.

PAGE DE GAUCHE :

Les guirlandes de verrines ont été réalisées par Alicia Goñi avec des pots de yaourt et du fil de fer.

À DROITE :

Les murs ont été peints en jaune et vert amande, les couleurs préférées de la maîtresse de maison qui affirme qu'elles embellissent avec le temps. Le vieux lit en fer est une relique familiale.

Alicia Goñi hat mit ihrer Geschäftspartnerin Florencia Pieres Cat Ballou geschaffen, eine Ladenkette für Kleider und Hausgegenstände, die wegen ihres freien und zwanglosen Stils bekannt sind. Alicia war es auch, die diese *rancho* ihrer Familie am Polo-Spielfeld Los Fresnos in der Provinz Buenos Aires umgestaltete. Der Ort ist traumhaft. Der Wohnsitz liegt ganz unauffällig in der Weite der Pampa. Er respektiert die Umgebung und passt sich dieser an. Um dem Bau einen antiken Charme zu verleihen, wurden Materialien aus Abrisshäusern verwendet, die bereits eine Patina besitzen: Alte Balken, Türen und Fenster geben dem Haus eine gewisse Authentizität. Dennoch ist die vorherrschende Atmosphäre hauptsächlich ein Resultat der verwendeten Farben und Texturen. „Mir gefällt es, alte Möbel wiederherzustellen und ihre Funktion zu ändern." Im Inneren des äußerlich sehr einfach wirkenden Hauses gibt es jede Menge Eleganz und Komfort – hier bringt Alicia ihre Talente als Dekorateurin und Malerin zum Ausdruck.

Connue pour avoir créé la chaîne de boutiques de meubles et de vêtements décontractés Cat Ballou avec son associée Florencia Pieres, Alicia Goñi a entrepris de retaper le *rancho* familial situé dans Los Fresnos, un vaste complexe de polo dans la province de Buenos Aires. Dans ce lieu de rêve au milieu de l'immensité de la pampa, la demeure répond à une consigne : respecter l'environnement et s'y intégrer. Pour lui donner l'air d'avoir toujours été là, elle fut construite avec des matériaux de démolition patinés par le temps. Poutres, portes et fenêtres lui confèrent une aura d'authenticité mais ce sont les couleurs et les textures qui créent l'atmosphère dominante. « J'aime récupérer de vieux meubles et les transformer. » Vue de l'extérieur, la maison paraît simple mais l'intérieur est une leçon d'élégance et de confort, Alicia Goñi y démontrant ses talents de décoratrice et de peintre.

ABOVE LEFT :
In the yard, the stable boys take great care of the mares.

BELOW LEFT :
Somewhere to rest in the shade: Provençal-style chairs stand side by side with rustic stools made from eucalyptus trunks.

RIGHT PAGE ABOVE:
In the garden, vegetables are grown to accompany asados (roast meat dishes) that are so popular on all Argentinian estancias (ranches).

RIGHT PAGE BELOW:
Polo team comprising prominent national and international players in action at Los Fresnos.

LINKS OBEN:
In den Ställen sorgen die peones (Landarbeiter) bestens für die Pferde.

LINKS UNTEN:
Für die Ruhepause im Schatten gibt es Stühle und Bänke im provenzalischen Stil neben rustikalen Sitzen und Tischen aus Eukalyptus-Baumstämmen.

RECHTE SEITE OBEN:
Im Garten wird Gemüse als Beilage zu asado (gegrilltem Fleisch) gezogen, das auf jeder argentinischen estancia in großen Mengen verzehrt wird.

RECHTE SEITE UNTEN:
Ein Team aus bekannten nationalen und internationalen Polospielern in Los Fresnos.

À GAUCHE, EN HAUT :
Devant les abreuvoirs, les palefreniers bichonnent les juments.

À GAUCHE, EN BAS :
Un coin tranquille à l'ombre. Des fauteuils de style provençal côtoient des tables rustiques faites de troncs d'eucalyptus.

PAGE DE DROITE, EN HAUT :
Le potager où l'on cultive les légumes pour accompagner les asados (grillades), plat de prédilection dans toutes les estancias argentines.

PAGE DE DROITE, EN BAS :
Une équipe de polo constituée d'éminents joueurs nationaux et internationaux réunis à Los Fresnos.

ALICIA GOÑI / GENERAL RODRÍGUEZ

Alicia Goñi loves the imperfect beauty of simple materials and untreated wood. The vintage iron stove is still in every-day use.

Alicia liebt die unvollkom-mene Schönheit und un-behandeltes Holz. Der alte Küchenherd aus Eisen wird jeden Tag genutzt.

Alicia Goñi aime la beauté imparfaite des matières et du bois bruts. La vieille cui-sinière en fonte fonctionne tous les jours.

150

LEFT PAGE:
Kitchen worktop detail, displaying a rustic, spartan simplicity.

RIGHT PAGE:
There is no boundary between kitchen and living room. Goñi has chosen cement floors, matt textures, rough wood and reclaimed furniture to give this house its style.

LINKE SEITE:
Die Küchenarbeitsfläche ist von spartanischer, rustikaler Einfachheit.

RECHTE SEITE:
Zwischen Küche und Wohnzimmer gibt es keine Abgrenzung. Betonboden, Texturen ohne Glanz, grobes Holz und restaurierte Möbel bilden den Stil, den die Designerin auf ihrer rancho einsetzt.

PAGE DE GAUCHE :
Détail du plan de travail de la cuisine, sa sobriété champêtre est d'une simplicité spartiate.

PAGE DE DROITE :
La cuisine est ouverte sur le salon. Sol en ciment, textures mates, bois brut et meubles de récupération.

152

ALICIA GOÑI / GENERAL RODRÍGUEZ

The rococo-style bed and
a handful of antiques that
belonged to Goñi's mother
bring a touch of sophis-
tication to this rustic
environment.

*Das Bett im Rokokostil und
einige antike Objekte, die
Alicias Mutter gehörten,
verleihen dem rustikalen
Ambiente einen Hauch
von Eleganz.*

*Dans ce décor rustique, le
lit de style rococo et quelques objets anciens qui
appartenaient à la mère
d'Alicia Goñi apportent une
touche de sophistication.*

154

156

ALICIA GOÑI / GENERAL RODRÍGUEZ

Las Calandrias

ANA MASSINI & EDUARDO AYERZA
SAN ANTONIO DE ARECO

This late 19th-century colonial-style house stands near San Antonio de Areco, the birthplace of the gaucho tradition. It is bordered by century-old trees and a strategic, orderly stand of cypresses that were the deciding factor when purchasing the property. A simple, low, white building but with plenty of character, the house bears the discrete but unmistakable hallmark of its owner, the antiquarian Ana Massini. English- and French-style furniture dominates the house, with special emphasis on certain classicist touches and an attachment to the bucolic tranquillity of nature, which serves as an ever-changing backdrop. "My house is not decorated; what I like is to be surrounded by my objects, my memories, the products of my life; some belonged to my family, others I bought at auctions," Massini explains. Mindful of the splendid setting and with a sensitive renovation of the exterior, she has created a cosy and inviting home for weekend retreats.

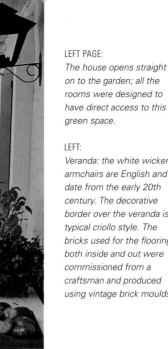

LEFT PAGE:

The house opens straight on to the garden; all the rooms were designed to have direct access to this green space.

LEFT:

Veranda: the white wicker armchairs are English and date from the early 20th century. The decorative border over the veranda is typical criollo style. The bricks used for the flooring both inside and out were commissioned from a craftsman and produced using vintage brick moulds.

LINKE SEITE:

Das Haus öffnet sich ungehindert zum Garten; alle Zimmer wurden mit direktem Ausgang ins Grüne entworfen.

LINKS:

Die weißen Korbstühle auf der Veranda stammen aus England und datieren vom Anfang des 20. Jahrhunderts. Den Bodenbelag aus Ziegeln in und außerhalb des Hauses schuf ein Handwerker nach alten Vorbildern.

PAGE DE GAUCHE :

La maison est entièrement tournée vers le jardin. Toutes les pièces donnent directement sur la verdure.

À GAUCHE :

Sur la véranda, des fauteuils anglais en rotin datant du début du 20ᵉ siècle. À l'intérieur comme à l'extérieur, les sols sont en briques fabriquées par un artisan avec des moules anciens.

Dieser Wohnsitz im Kolonialstil vom Ende des 19. Jahrhunderts liegt in der Nähe von San Antonio de Areco, der Wiege der Gaucho-Tradition. Beim Kauf des Anwesens waren die uralten Bäume, die das Grundstück umgeben, und vor allem die geschickte Anordnung der Zypressen von entscheidender Bedeutung. Das Haus ist ein einfacher, weißer lang gestreckter Bau, der unverwechselbar von seiner Besitzerin, der Antiquitätenhändlerin Ana Massini, geprägt ist. Möbel im englischen und französischen Stil dominieren, doch kommen bestimmte klassizistische Noten ebenso zum Ausdruck wie die Neigung zur bukolischen Stille der Natur. „Mein Haus ist nicht designt, denn ich sehe mich gern umgeben von meinen Andenken und Erinnerungen, den Früchten des Lebens; einige sind Familienbesitz, andere habe ich bei Versteigerungen gekauft", meint Massini, die mit einem Umbau, der die prachtvolle Umgebung mit einbezog, ein bezauberndes Wochenendhaus schuf.

Située près de San Antonio de Areco, berceau de la tradition gaucho, cette demeure coloniale de la fin du 19ᵉ siècle est ceinte d'arbres centenaires, notamment des rangées stratégiquement ordonnées de cyprès qui jouèrent un rôle déterminant dans la décision d'acheter la propriété. La bâtisse de plain-pied, sobre, blanche et riche en nuances, porte l'empreinte discrète et unique de la maîtresse de maison, l'antiquaire Ana Massini. Les meubles de styles anglais et français prédominent, apportant des touches de classicisme dans une ambiance faisant la part belle aux attraits bucoliques de la nature. Cette dernière crée des tableaux toujours changeants qu'encadrent les fenêtres. « Ma maison n'est pas décorée », explique Mme Massini. « J'aime être entourée de mes souvenirs, des objets qui ont compté dans ma vie. Certains viennent de ma famille, d'autres ont été achetés dans des ventes aux enchères. » Tirant le meilleur parti de ce havre splendide, en parfaite communion avec le grand air, elle a su créer une maison de campagne au charme irrésistible.

LEFT PAGE ABOVE:
A bookcase dominates the living room. The dining room has a butcher's block table and late 19th-century French chairs upholstered in toile de Jouy fabric.

LEFT PAGE BELOW:
Bedroom with flower engravings, English cabinets and bedside tables and the original window grille.

ABOVE RIGHT:
The old, twin-oven cast iron kitchen range is used regularly in winter. The splashback is made of floor tiles.

ABOVE RIGHT:
The living room is simple and traditional with a wood-beamed ceiling.

LINKE SEITE OBEN:
Dominierendes Element des Wohnzimmers ist die Bücherwand. An einem Metzgertisch stehen französische Stühle vom Ende des 19. Jahrhunderts mit Bezügen aus toile de Jouy.

LINKE SEITE UNTEN:
Im Schlafzimmer hängen an der Wand französische Blumenstiche und Spiegel mit Konsolen, neben den Betten stehen englische Nachttische, und vor dem Fenster sind noch die originalen Gitter zu sehen.

RECHTS OBEN:
In der Küche ist die Wand mit Ziegeln verkleidet. Der alte Herd aus Gusseisen mit doppeltem Backrohr wird vor allem im Winter fleißig genutzt.

RECHTS UNTEN:
Die Decke des Wohn- und Esszimmers ist mit Holzbalken verkleidet.

PAGE DE GAUCHE, EN HAUT :
La salle à manger est aménagée avec une table de boucher et des chaises françaises de la fin du 19ᵉ siècle tapissée de toile de Jouy.

PAGE DE GAUCHE, EN BAS :
Dans la chambre les gravures de fleurs. Miroirs-consoles et tables de chevet anglaises. Les grilles sont d'origine.

À DROITE, EN HAUT :
La vieille cuisinière en fonte à deux fours sert surtout en hiver. Le sol est en briques.

À DROITE, EN BAS :
Le séjour avec des poutres apparentes.

LAS CALANDRIAS / SAN ANTONIO DE ARECO

La Esperanza

PILAR

"We planned this house mindful of the lie of the land, the intensity of the rain, the direction of the wind. We designed it intuitively, like birds or insects, according to the proximity of the water and the trees, considering the landscape as a whole," explain these architects and interior designers who describe themselves first and foremost as "country people." Through their interpretation of the brief given by the owner – a man in love with the Argentine countryside – Gonzalo Córdoba and Carlos Alberto Pepe have recaptured the spirit of the old houses of the *pampa*. The brilliant result is a single-storey building with a side wing and verandas on both sides to provide protection from the wind and made of fine, solid materials. The old *quebracho* wood beams and ceramic roof tiling found on most of the roofs, the *pinotea* wood floors, mud bricks, mosaic work, cast iron artefacts, tall, old openings and large fireplaces, give it solidity and character. "These materials were collected with the perseverance of a tracker who observes and interprets the marks left behind, looking for signs of the story they tell," the architects explain.

LEFT PAGE:
View of one side of the house, with two enamelled metal lamps of the kind commonly used to light the front of country barns.

RIGHT:
Block at the end of the veranda, housing the main bedroom.

FOLLOWING DOUBLE PAGE:
Front of the house painted in coloured lime wash made from natural dye and central veranda supported by hand-hewn carob tree trunks from the north of Argentina.

LINKE SEITE:
Eine Seite des Hauses mit zwei Lampen aus emailliertem Blech, die ansonsten zur Beleuchtung von Feldscheunen dienen.

RECHTS:
In einem vorstehenden Baukörper, der auf einer Seite die Veranda flankiert, ist das Hauptschlafzimmer untergebracht.

FOLGENDE DOPPELSEITE:
Frontseite des Hauses, das mit Kalkfarbe aus natürlichen Pigmenten gestrichen wurde. Die Säulen der Veranda wurden aus nordargentinischem Johannisbrotbaum-Holz von Hand geschnitzt.

PAGE DE GAUCHE :
Un des côtés de la maison avec deux lampes extérieures en tôle émaillée, généralement utilisées pour illuminer les façades des hangars à la campagne.

À DROITE :
Une des ailes de la maison qui abrite la chambre principale.

DOUBLE PAGE SUIVANTE :
La façade de la maison avec ses murs peints à la chaux teintée avec des pigments naturels. La galerie est soutenue par des colonnes en caroubier taillées à la main et provenant du nord de l'Argentine.

163

„Als wir dieses Haus entwarfen, berücksichtigten wir den Einfall der Sonne, die Intensität des Regens und des Winds. Wir haben intuitiv gebaut, wie die Vögel und die Insekten, im Einklang mit dem nahen Wasser und den Bäumen und mit Verständnis für die Natur insgesamt", berichten die Architekten und Designer, die sich selbst als „Landmenschen" bezeichnen. Gonzalo Córdoba und Carlos Alberto Pepe interpretierten die Vorstellungen des Hausherrn, eines Anhängers des argentinischen Landlebens, indem sie den Geist der alten Häuser in der Pampa wieder zum Leben erweckten. Ein einziges Geschoss mit einem Flügel, Veranden zu beiden Seiten als Schutz vor den Winden sowie edle und solide Materialien waren das gelungene Ergebnis. Alte *quebracho*-Balken und Tonziegel für die meisten Dächer, Böden aus Fichtenholz, Lehmziegel, Mosaiken, Artefakte aus Gusseisen und großzügige Kamine verliehen dem Haus Solidität und Charakter. „Diese Materialien wurden mit der Beharrlichkeit eines Fährtenlesers zusammengetragen, der Spuren verfolgt und analysiert und auf der Suche nach den Zeichen der Geschichte ist", bekräftigen die Architekten.

« Nous avons conçu cette maison en tenant compte de l'incidence du sol, de l'intensité des pluies et du parcours des vents », expliquent Gonzalo Córdoba et Carlos Alberto Pepe, deux architectes/décorateurs qui se définissent avant tout comme « des hommes de la campagne ». « Nous travaillons intuitivement, comme les oiseaux et les insectes, en fonction de la proximité de l'eau et des arbres, en intégrant le paysage dans son ensemble. » Interprétant l'idée du propriétaire, un amoureux du *campo* argentin, ils ont recréé l'esprit des vieilles demeures de la pampa : un bâtiment de plain-pied, avec deux ailes latérales protégées du vent par des galeries, des matériaux nobles et robustes, de vieilles poutres en *quebracho*, des tuiles en céramique sur le toit, des parquets en sapin, des briques en torchis, du carrelage, de la fonte, des grandes cheminées partout. « Tous ces matériaux ont été récupérés avec la persévérance d'un traqueur qui observe et analyse les traces, cherchant des signes de l'histoire. »

PREVIOUS PAGE LEFT:
Living room and dining room with pinotea wood floors. Over the fireplace is a cardon (cactus) wood lintel.

PREVIOUS PAGE RIGHT:
The kitchen has a clay tile floor; the old pinotea wood cupboard was rescued from an old store.

LEFT PAGE:
The bathroom with floor in a chequered design and vintage tiles on the walls.

RIGHT PAGE:
The main bedroom with a bedside table made from cardon (cactus) wood. On the bed is a guanaco hide rug.

VORIGE SEITE LINKS:
Wohn- und Esszimmer haben Böden aus Fichtenholz. Der Kamin ist von dem Stamm eines Cardón-Kaktus bekrönt.

VORIGE SEITE RECHTS:
Lehmfliesen in der Küche. Die alte Anrichte aus Fichtenholz wurde aus einem alten Lagerhaus gerettet.

LINKE SEITE:
Im Badezimmer wurde der Boden schachbrettartig mit Fliesen verlegt. Die Wand ist mit alten Keramikfliesen geschmückt.

RECHTE SEITE:
Der Nachttisch im Schlafzimmer besteht aus Cardón-Kaktus. Auf dem Bett liegt eine Decke aus Guanakofell.

PAGE PRÉCÉDENTE, À GAUCHE :
Séjour et salle à manger, avec un parquet en sapin. La cheminée est couronnée par un tronc de cactus.

PAGE PRÉCÉDENTE, À DROITE :
Dans la cuisine, un sol en dalles de terre cuite. Le comptoir en sapin a été récupéré dans une vieille épicerie.

PAGE DE GAUCHE :
La salle de bains avec un sol en damier et carreaux en faïence anciens.

PAGE DE DROITE :
Dans la chambre principale, une table de chevet en cactus. Sur le lit, une couverture en fourrure de guanaco.

168

La Escondida

FLORENCIA & PAUL PIERES

PILAR

Less than an hour's drive from the centre of Buenos Aires stands La Escondida (the Hidden One), the *estancia* of Florencia and Paul Pieres. Paul is a well-known polo player. His wife, Florencia, is an interior designer and has made their house into an oasis of peace. The building was designed by architect Pablo Sanchez Elía. With its strict symmetry and simple lines, the building blends subtly, almost anonymously, into the tones of the surrounding landscape. The walls are painted in earth tones and the blue of the pool rivals the green of nature. With just a handful of flowers and a profusion of flax and herb plants, landscape designer Carlos Thays has succeeded in creating a garden that is somewhere between cultivated and wild. The interior of the house was designed as a space with as few divisions as possible, with smooth walls, and doors reaching up to the roof with no upper frame, giving a sense of restrained, elegant spaciousness. The result reflects the current trend in country homes: discrete integration with the environment, an intelligent appreciation of tradition, elegant simplicity and, of course, relaxing views over the surrounding land.

LEFT PAGE:
Ideal for lovers of nature and equestrian sports, a property where country pursuits are very popular.

LEFT:
The lack of architectural distractions helps to integrate the dwelling into its environment.

LINKE SEITE:
Liebhaber der Natur und des Reitsports können auf der estancia La Escondida unterschiedlichen Freizeitaktivitäten nachgehen.

LINKS:
Das Fehlen von architektonischen Extravaganzen trägt dazu bei, dass sich der Landsitz in die Umgebung integriert.

PAGE DE GAUCHE :
Parmi les nombreuses activités champêtres, la propriété a de quoi ravir les amoureux de la nature et des sports équestres.

À GAUCHE :
La sobriété de l'architecture aide la bâtisse à s'intégrer dans son environnement.

Eine knappe Autostunde vom Zentrum von Buenos Aires entfernt liegt La Escondida, die *Estancia* des Ehepaars Pieres. Paul ist ein berühmter Polospieler, und seine Frau Florencia machte als Designerin ihren Wohnsitz zu einer Oase der Ruhe. Das Haus ist ein Projekt des Architekten Pablo Sanchez Elía. Mit der strengen Symmetrie und den einfachen Linien ist das Bauwerk auf diskrete, fast anonyme Weise in Farben und Formen der natürlichen Umgebung eingebettet. Die Wände sind in Erdfarben gehalten, und das Blau des Swimmingpools wetteifert mit dem Grün der Landschaft. Der Landschaftsgärtner Carlos Thays legte einen teils natürlichwilden, teils kultivierten Garten an. Die schlichten Räume sind nur sparsam durch Mauern unterteilt und haben fast deckenhohe, rahmenlose Türen, um zurückhaltende und elegante Weiträumigkeit auszustrahlen. Das Ergebnis spiegelt die aktuellen Trends für Landhäuser: unauffällige Verschmelzung mit der Natur, kluge Wertschätzung der Tradition, elegante Schlichtheit und natürlich einige erholsame Ausblicke auf die Landschaft.

La Escondida, l'*estancia* des Pieres, se trouve à moins d'une heure de voiture du centre de Buenos Aires. Paul est un célèbre joueur de polo. Son épouse, Florencia, décoratrice, a transformé leur demeure en havre de tranquillité. D'apparence simple et austère, la maison fut bâtie par l'architecte Pablo Sanchez Elía. Avec sa symétrie rigoureuse et ses lignes sobres, elle se fond discrètement dans la nature. Ses murs sont peints couleur terre et le bleu de la piscine rivalise avec la verdure environnante. Dans le jardin, le paysagiste Carlos Thays est parvenu, avec peu de fleurs et une profusion de lins et d'herbes folles, à conjuguer le formel et le sauvage. À l'intérieur, les espaces sont le moins compartimenté possible. Des murs lisses et des portes qui vont du sol au plafond apportent une amplitude dépouillée et élégante. La demeure illustre parfaitement la tendance actuelle en matière de maisons de campagne : une intégration discrète dans l'environnement, une revalorisation savante de la tradition, une simplicité raffinée et, naturellement, des vues reposantes sur la campagne.

172

ABOVE LEFT:
Horses are a passion for the Pieres family.

BELOW LEFT:
The long rectangle of the swimming pool is a haven of peace in the midst of fertile land.

RIGHT PAGE ABOVE:
The swimming pool reflects the stillness of the sky and forms the perfect prelude to the interior. "Its long, narrow form, designed for swimming, is also a place of passage for guests arriving and leaving."

RIGHT PAGE BELOW:
The outdoor dining area is constructed from tree trunks draped in climbing jasmines; the furniture is of plain, rustic wood.

LINKS OBEN:
Pferde sind die Leidenschaft der Familie Pieres.

UNTEN LINKS:
Das lang gezogene Rechteck des Swimmingpools ist eine Oase des Friedens inmitten des fruchtbaren Landes.

RECHTE SEITE OBEN:
Der Swimmingpool, der die Stille des Himmels spiegelt, stimmt perfekt auf das Eintreten ins Haus ein. „Seine lange, schmale zum Schwimmen geeignete Form ist auch Zeuge des Kommens und Gehens der Gäste."

RECHTE SEITE UNTEN:
Der Essplatz im Freien wurde aus Baumstämmen konstruiert, an denen sich Jasmin emporrankt; die einfachen und rustikalen Möbel bestehen aus Holz.

À GAUCHE, EN HAUT :
La famille Pieres a la passion des chevaux.

À GAUCHE, EN BAS :
La longue piscine est un havre de paix au milieu des terres fécondes.

PAGE DE DROITE, EN HAUT :
La piscine, qui reflète le ciel serein, est la prolongation parfaite de l'intérieur de la maison. « Etroite et longue, elle est conçue pour nager. »

PAGE DE DROITE, EN BAS :
La salle à manger extérieure est abritée sous une pergola en troncs d'arbres sur lesquels grimpent des jasmins. Les meubles simples sont en bois rustique.

PREVIOUS DOUBLE PAGE:
Architecture in a modern vernacular where strict simplicity becomes a homage to light, serenity and space.

ABOVE LEFT:
The building extends over 200 square metres and has cleverly designed passageways.

BELOW LEFT:
Ceiling with hand-crafted bricks and exposed beams. Around the table are old family chairs that have been reclaimed and re-upholstered.

RIGHT PAGE:
Elegant details are also found in the kitchen. Florencia has used local wood for the kitchen furniture and upholstered the door in leather. She enjoys a reputation as an excellent cook and hostess.

VORIGE DOPPELSEITE:
Eine Architektur in moderner Sprache, deren Strenge eine Huldigung an das Licht, die Heiterkeit und den Raum ist.

LINKS OBEN:
Das Gebäude erstreckt sich über 200 Quadratmeter Grundfläche und hat eine gut durchdachte Aufteilung.

LINKS UNTEN:
Die Zimmerdecke aus handgeformten Ziegeln und sichtbaren Deckenbalken. Um den Tisch sind alte Stühle aus Familienbesitz gruppiert, die restauriert und neu bezogen wurden.

RECHTE SEITE:
Elegante Details auch in der Küche. Florencia verwendete einheimisches Holz für die Möbel und verkleidete die Tür mit Leder. Sie genießt den Ruf, eine gute Köchin und eine ausgezeichnete Gastgeberin zu sein.

DOUBLE PAGE PRÉCÉDENTE :
Une architecture moderne où la rigueur devient une ode à la lumière, à la sérénité et à l'espace.

À GAUCHE, EN HAUT :
La construction couvre 200 mètres carrés et jouit d'une circulation bien étudiée.

À GAUCHE, EN BAS :
Faux plafond réalisé avec des planches artisanales et des poutres apparentes. Autour de la table, des chaises anciennes récupérées dans la famille et retapissées.

PAGE DE DROITE :
Détails élégants dans la cuisine. Pour les meubles, Florencia Pieres a utilisé des bois locaux. La porte est tapissée de cuir. Elle a la réputation d'être un cordon bleu et une excellente hôtesse.

LA ESCONDIDA / PILAR

ABOVE LEFT:
Console table made of lenga, a native wood from the south of Argentina and a protected species which can only be collected at certain times of year. There are fresh garden flowers throughout the house.

BELOW LEFT:
The bathroom is partially integrated into the bedroom and gives the sense of being part of a single space.

RIGHT PAGE ABOVE:
The living room with comfortable, homely armchairs and sofa in pink upholstery positioned around the fireplace.

RIGHT PAGE BELOW:
In the bedrooms, white linen is used with natural, coloured fabrics as bedspreads and curtains.

LINKS OBEN:
Konsolentisch aus lenga, einem Gehölz aus Südargentinien, das unter Naturschutz steht und nur zu bestimmten Jahreszeiten gesammelt werden kann. Überall stehen frische Blumen aus dem Garten.

LINKS UNTEN:
Das Bad geht teilweise in das Schlafzimmer über und vermittelt den Eindruck, Teil des Raums zu sein.

RECHTE SEITE OBEN:
Im Wohnzimmer stehen bequeme Sessel und Sofas mit rosa Bezügen um den Kamin.

RECHTE SEITE UNTEN:
Im Schlafzimmer wurden weißes Leinen und Stoffe in natürlichen Farben für Bettüberwürfe und Vorhänge verwendet.

À GAUCHE, EN HAUT :
Une console réalisée dans un bois du sud de l'Argentine ; l'espèce, protégée, ne peut être abattue que certains mois de l'année. Partout, des fleurs fraîches du jardin.

À GAUCHE, EN BAS :
La salle de bains est partiellement intégrée à la chambre, créant l'illusion d'un seul espace.

PAGE DE DROITE, EN HAUT :
Devant la cheminée du salon, de confortables fauteuils de famille houssés de rose.

PAGE DE DROITE, EN BAS :
Dans les chambres, les couvre-lits et les rideaux sont en lin blanc ou en tissus aux tons naturels.

LA ESCONDIDA / PILAR

ENERGÍA

NECOCHEA

In Buenos Aires Province, five hours down the motorway heading south, one encounters a surprising and impressive landscape of dunes and cliffs. Pine trees, pampas grass, rheas, whales on their coastal route to Puerto Madryn and the occasional stray penguin inhabit these wild places. It was here on an old *estancia* that one couple decided to create a home and commissioned Pablo Sanchez Elía and Laura Orcoyen to make their dreams a reality. The result is a large house built in stone from Mar del Plata – the nearest quarry in the area – where every element is in harmony with its surroundings and the spirit of the place. Access is via a pine wood that provides protection and shelter from the strong winds. The front of the house opens on to the sea and the dunes. In the interior, the stone, treated pine and pale tones blend with the landscape; the decking terrace, small pool and fireplace create a transition towards the sea. Laura Orcoyen has decorated the house with canopied beds, large, stripped-wood wardrobes and cupboards, natural textures and pale colours.

LEFT PAGE:
The façade facing the sea, constructed in Mar del Plata stone and built on 3 different levels, following the contours of the land.

LEFT:
Elements from the nature that surrounds the house are incorporated into the architecture of the building – like this pool of water on the decking.

LINKE SEITE:
Der Höhenunterschied in der Hausfront, die sich dem Meer öffnet, ist auf das Gefälle im Grundstück zurückzuführen.

LINKS:
Ein Beispiel für die Einbeziehung von Naturelementen in die Architektur: das Wasserbecken auf der Holzterrasse.

PAGE DE GAUCHE :
La façade donnant sur la mer, en pierres de Mar del Plata, épouse le relief du terrain en jouant sur trois niveaux.

À GAUCHE :
Un exemple de l'intégration des éléments naturels dans l'architecture de la maison : un bassin percé dans la terrasse en bois.

In der Provinz Buenos Aires, fünf Autostunden in Richtung Süden, überrascht den Besucher eine eindrucksvolle Landschaft aus Dünen und Steilküsten. Kiefern, Pampagras, Nandus, Wale im Meer oder ein verirrter Pinguin beleben die Gegend auf dem Weg nach Puerto Madryn. Hier beauftragte ein Ehepaar mit einer alten *Estancia* aus Familienbesitz Pablo Sanchez Elía und Laura Orcoyen mit der Realisierung ihrer Träume. Das Ergebnis war ein aus Steinen von Mar del Plata – dem nächsten Steinbruch – gemauertes Haus, ganz im Einklang mit der Umgebung. Der Zugang durch eine Fichtengruppe bietet Schutz gegen die starken Winde. Die Hausfront selbst öffnet sich zum Meer und zu den Dünen. Die Steine, das Fichtenholz und die hellen Farben im Inneren verschmelzen mit der Landschaft; auf der Holzterrasse bilden das kleine Wasserbecken und der offene Kamin einen Übergang zum Meer. Die Einrichtung mit den Himmelbetten, den großen gebeizten Schränken, den natürlichen Materialien und den hellen Farben gestaltete Laura Orcoyen.

Dans la province de Buenos Aires, à cinq heures de route vers le sud, un imposant paysage de dunes et de falaises borde la côte. Ce coin sauvage est peuplé de pins, d'herbes de la Pampa, de nandous, de baleines en route vers Puerto Madryn et parfois d'un pingouin égaré. C'est là, dans une vieille *estancia* familiale, qu'un couple a demandé à Pablo Sanchez Elía et à Laura Orcoyen de créer la maison de leurs rêves. La grande structure en pierres de Mar del Plata (la carrière la plus proche) épouse le relief et regarde vers la mer. Chaque recoin a été pensé en fonction de l'environnement et de l'esprit du lieu. On y accède en traversant une forêt de pins qui protège des vents puissants. À l'intérieur, la pierre, le pin traité et les tons clairs se fondent dans le paysage. Sur la terrasse en bois, un bassin et un foyer assurent la transition vers l'océan. Laura Orcoyen a décoré l'intérieur avec des lits à baldaquin, de grandes armoires décapées et des textures naturelles.

182

ABOVE LEFT:
The stone fireplace is an important spot where the family comes together, in close contact with nature.

BELOW LEFT:
Living room with a curved sofa designed by Laura Orcoyen and a chinaberry table.

RIGHT PAGE ABOVE:
The outdoor fireplace at sunset with organically-formed table and bench from the north of Argentina.

RIGHT PAGE BELOW:
Living room with the kitchen beyond, seen from the terrace. The neocriollo-style furnishing was designed by Laura Orcoyen and is a fusion of European furniture and Argentinian materials.

LINKS OBEN:
Der offene Steinkamin ist ein wichtiger Treffpunkt der Familie, die sehr naturverbunden ist.

LINKS UNTEN:
Im Wohnzimmer ein geschwungenes Sofa nach einem Entwurf von Laura Orcoyen, in der Mitte ein Tisch aus nordargentinischem paraiso-Holz.

RECHTE SEITE OBEN:
Der gemauerte Kamin bei Sonnenuntergang, mit organisch geformtem Tisch und Bank aus nordargentinischem Holz.

RECHTE SEITE UNTEN:
Das Wohnzimmer und die Küche im Hintergrund, von der Terrasse aus gesehen. Das von Laura gestaltete Mobiliar im estilo neocriollo (neukreolischen Stil) mischt europäische Möbel mit argentinischen Materialien.

À GAUCHE, EN HAUT :
La grande cheminée en pierre sur la terrasse, devant laquelle la famille se réunit souvent.

À GAUCHE, EN BAS :
Dans le séjour, un canapé arrondi de Laura Orcoyen, une table basse en bois paraiso.

PAGE DE DROITE, EN HAUT :
La cheminée extérieure au coucher de soleil. Table et banc aux formes organiques provenant du nord de l'Argentine.

PAGE DE DROITE, EN BAS :
Le séjour, avec la cuisine au fond, vu depuis la terrasse. Le mobilier neocriollo de Laura Orcoyen, mêle le style européen et les matériaux argentins.

LEFT PAGE:
The master bedroom situated on the upper floor, with canopied bed and stone bathtub beyond. The dominant colours of the landscape are echoed in the walls, fabrics and furniture.

RIGHT PAGE:
Living room with Ricardo Paz table from the north of Argentina and French Louis XV-style chairs re-upholstered in foal hide.

LINKE SEITE:
Im Schlafzimmer des Obergeschosses ist im Hintergrund eine steinerne Badewanne zu sehen. Die vorherrschenden Farben der Landschaft wurden für die Wände, die Stoffe und das Mobiliar übernommen.

RECHTE SEITE:
Im Wohnzimmer ein Tisch aus nordargentinischem Holz von Ricardo Paz sowie französische Sessel im Stil Louis XV., mit Fohlenleder neu bezogen.

PAGE DE GAUCHE :
La chambre principale au premier étage. Derrière le lit à baldaquin, une baignoire en pierre. On retrouve les couleurs du paysage sur les murs, les tissus et le mobilier.

PAGE DE DROITE :
Dans le séjour, une table de Ricardo Paz dans un bois du nord de l'Argentine. Fauteuils français de style Louis XV retapissés en cuir de poulain.

186

ABOVE LEFT:
Stone bathroom located on the upper floor and continuing the same colour palette found throughout the house.

BELOW LEFT:
Behind the bed, set into one of the walls, is a fireplace in stone from the Mar del Plata quarry.

RIGHT PAGE:
The kitchen adjoins the living room but is separated by gauze curtains. The same fusion of fine materials continues here too with the use of steel.

LINKS OBEN:
Das Bad aus Stein im Obergeschoss fügt sich in die vorherrschende Farbpalette des Hauses ein.

LINKS UNTEN:
Hinter dem Bett ist ein gemauerter Kamin zu sehen, die Steine stammen aus dem Steinbruch in Mar del Plata.

RECHTE SEITE:
In der vom Wohnzimmer durch Gazevorhänge abgetrennten Küche wird die gelungene Zusammenstellung der Materialien auch im Einsatz von Edelstahl offensichtlich.

À GAUCHE, EN HAUT :
La baignoire en pierre, située à l'étage, reste conforme à la palette ocre et sable du reste de la maison.

À GAUCHE, EN BAS :
Derrière le lit de l'une des chambres, une cheminée en pierres de Mar del Plata.

PAGE DE DROITE :
Dans la cuisine, séparée du séjour par un voilage en gaze, la noblesse de l'acier.

Susana Gronda

VOLCÁN

Night falls and clouds trail low across the landscape. Up above rise the graceful peaks of the Quebrada Chilcayoc mountains. This is Volcán, in the old province of Jujuy in the north of Argentina. And it is here that the artist, writer and architect Susana Gronda decided to create a retreat on a *finca* that had been in the hands of her family since 1602, building on the foundations of a former shepherds' hut. The construction is simple, based on colonial lines, intuitively executed by local people, with simple touches of popular local architecture and with the splendour of nature permeating throughout. A spring rising in the mountains winds its way across the small, covered patio that divides the main living room space and adobe-walled kitchen from the bedroom and bathroom. Simple, leather-strutted camp beds for sleeping, mortars for grinding corn, rustic *bateas* and *pozuelos* (trays and troughs) for storing towels and sheets are among the few objects found in these small spaces. When night falls, the candlelight, the warmth of the fire and sound of the wind take us back to a more distant rural past.

LEFT PAGE:
Stones blocks that were once the lintels of the old buildings that stood on this site.

LEFT:
This old, mud- and stone-built structure is now used to house the car.

LINKE SEITE:
Die Steinblöcke dienten einst als Türstürze in alten Bauten des Ortes.

LINKS:
Das Gebäude aus Stein und Lehm wird heute als Stellplatz für das Auto genutzt.

PAGE DE GAUCHE :
Ces blocs de pierre qui rappellent des sculptures étaient autrefois des linteaux de bâtisses aujourd'hui disparues.

À GAUCHE :
Une vieille construction en pierres sèches renforcée avec de la boue, qui sert désormais de garage.

Wenn in der Ortschaft Volcán in der nordargentinischen Provinz Jujuy die Dämmerung hereinbricht, leuchten die Gipfel der Chilcayoc-Berge. Hier schuf sich die Malerin, Schriftstellerin und Architektin Susana Gronda ihr Refugium in einer Finca, die sich seit 1602 im Besitz ihrer Familie befindet und auf den Grundmauern eines alten Steinhauses steht. Der Bau ist schlicht, die Silhouette erinnert an kolonialzeitliche Gebäude, während die Bauweise selbst uralten lokalen Traditionen verpflichtet ist und große Naturverbundenheit aufweist. Eine aus den Bergen kommende Quelle fließt durch den kleinen überdachten Patio, der das Wohnzimmer und die Küche aus *adobe* (luftgetrockneten Lehmziegeln) von Bad und Schlafzimmer trennt. Pritschen zum Schlafen, Mörser zum Mahlen der Maiskörner, *bateas* und *pozuelos* (Truhen) zur Aufbewahrung von Handtüchern und Bettwäsche sind einige der wenigen Objekte, die die kleinen Räume beleben. Wenn es Nacht wird, versetzen das Kerzenlicht, die Wärme des Feuers und das Rauschen des Windes die Bewohner in eine ferne Vergangenheit.

Le soir tombe et les pics altiers qui dominent la Quebrada Chilcayoc percent le bas plafond nuageux. C'est dans ce paysage de la province de Jujuy, dans la localité de Volcán, que l'artiste, écrivain et architecte Susana Gronda a créé son refuge dans une *finca* appartenant à sa famille depuis 1602. Elle est construite sur les fondations d'anciennes maisons de bergers, avec des murs en adobe ou en pierres sèches consolidées avec de la boue. La maison, simple, à la silhouette coloniale, répond à la logique intuitive des constructions autochtones, avec des touches ingénieuses typiques de l'architecture populaire. Ici, la chaleur est fournie par les feux de bois, la lumière provient des bougies et la nature pénètre à l'intérieur dans toute sa splendeur. Un ruisseau jaillit de la montagne et traverse la cour protégée d'un toit qui sépare le séjour et la cuisine de la chambre. Dans celle-ci, de petites ouvertures dans les murs en pierre laissent filtrer la lumière. Le mobilier, dépouillé, est constitué de lits sanglés de lanières de cuir, de mortiers pour moudre le maïs et de bassines en bois pour ranger le linge, autant d'objets qui nous renvoient à un passé lointain.

PREVIOUS DOUBLE PAGE:
The buildings, constructed of mud and stone, and the irrigation pool. In the background, the Quebrada Chilcayoc mountains.

LEFT PAGE:
View from the kitchen which opens on to the living room: the walls are made of mud, the uprights are carob wood and the ceiling is cardon (a type of cactus from the north of Argentina) and poplar.

RIGHT PAGE:
The living room with stone walls, a mud-built fireplace and smoothed cement floors coloured ochre and red.

VORIGE DOPPELSEITE:
Das Haus wurde aus Steinen und Lehm errichtet, im Vordergrund ein Wasserreservoir und dahinter die Chilcayoc-Berge.

LINKE SEITE:
Blick aus der Küche ins Wohnzimmer: Die Wände sind aus Lehm, die Säulen aus dem Holz des Johannisbrotbaums und die Dachbalken aus Cardón-Kaktus und Pappelholz.

194

RECHTE SEITE:
Der Kamin im Wohnzimmer ist aus Lehm geformt; dem Zement der Böden wurden ockerfarbene und rote Pigmente beigemischt.

DOUBLE PAGE PRÉCÉDENTE :
La maison, construite avec des pierres de la montagne, et l'étang. Derrière, la Quebrada Chilcayoc.

PAGE DE GAUCHE :
La cuisine, ouverte sur le séjour. Les murs sont en adobe. La charpente est en peuplier et en cactus.

PAGE DE DROITE :
La cheminée du séjour, en terre. Le sol est en ciment lissé coloré avec des pigments ocre et rouges.

SUSANA GRONDA / VOLCÁN

The bedroom is built of stone and coloured mud dyed with natural pigments. On the beds and floor are aguayos (woven throws) and the squat wooden chairs have goatskin seats.

Das Schlafzimmer hat Steinwände, die teilweise mit natürlich gefärbtem Lehm verputzt sind. Auf den Betten liegen aguayos, und vor dem Kamin stehen Holzstühle, deren Sitzflächen mit Ziegenleder bespannt sind.

La chambre, avec des murs en pierres et torchis. Sur le lit et au sol, des tapis aguayos. Chaises materas tendues de cuir.

196

Addresses / Adressen / Adresses

ARQUITECTOS (ARCHITECTS)

ESTUDIO DE ARQUITECTURA
Pablo Sanchez Elía
Ramsay 2414
1428 Buenos Aires
Argentina
PHONE: +54 11 4788-2889
EMAIL: estudio@pablosanchezelia.com.ar

ESTUDIO PAC
Costa Rica 5646
1414 Buenos Aires
Argentina
PHONE: +54 11 4772-6871
EMAIL: pac1@fibertel.com.ar
www.pacweb.com.ar

MACHADO AND SILVETTI ASSOCIATES
Rodolfo Machado & Jorge Silvetti
560 Harrison Avenue
Boston, Massachusetts 02118
USA
PHONE: +1 617 426 7070
EMAIL: info@machado-silvetti.com
www.machado-silvetti.com

DISEÑADORES (DESIGNERS)

LAURA O.
Laura Ocampo
Godoy Cruz 1575
1414 Buenos Aires
Argentina
PHONE: +54 11 4778-9550
EMAIL: tep@laurao.com
www.laurao.com

RICARDO PAZ
El Salvador 4656
1414 Buenos Aires
Argentina
PHONE: +54 11 4832-0516
EMAIL: rpaz@ricardopaz.com
www.ricardopaz.com

HOTEL

LA ESCONDIDA
Polo Lodges
Florencia & Paul Pieres
Chacras de Murray
Ruta 28, km 7.5
1629 Pilar
Provincia de Buenos Aires
Argentina
PHONE: +54 2322-400588
EMAIL: info@paulpieres.com
www.estancialaescondida.com.ar

FAENA HOTEL + UNIVERSE
Martha Salotti 445
Dique 2 Puerto Madero Este
1107 Buenos Aires
Argentina
PHONE: +54 11 4010-9000
EMAIL: info@faenaexperience.com
www.faenahotelanduniverse.com

RESTAURANTES (RESTAURANTS)

CONFITERÍA IDEAL
Suipacha 380
1008 Buenos Aires
Argentina
PHONE: +54 11 5265-8069
www.confiteriaideal.com

OLSEN
Chef: Germán Martitegui
Gorriti 5870
1414 Buenos Aires
Argentina
PHONE: +54 11 4776-7677
EMAIL: olsen@fibertel.com.ar

PATAGONIA SUR
Chef: Francis Mallmann
Rocha 823
1166 Buenos Aires
Argentina
PHONE: +54 11 4303-5917
EMAIL: info@restaurantepatagoniasur.com
www.restaurantepatagoniasur.com

MUSEOS (MUSEUMS)

MUSEO XUL SOLAR
Laprida 1212
1425 Buenos Aires
Argentina
PHONE: +54 11 4824-3302
EMAIL: info@xulsolar.org.ar
www.xulsolar.org.ar

VILLA OCAMPO
Elortondo 1837
1643 Beccar, Partido de San Isidro
Provincia de Buenos Aires
Argentina
PHONE: +54 11 4732-4988
EMAIL: informes@villaocampo.org
www.villaocampo.org

TEATRO (THEATRE)

TEATRO COLÓN
Cerrito 618
1010 Buenos Aires
Argentina
PHONE: +54 11 4378-7344
EMAIL: informaciones_colon@buenosaires.gov.ar
www.teatrocolon.org.ar

TIENDAS (SHOPS)

CAT BALLOU
Alicia Goñi & Florencia Pieres
Chacras de Murray
Ruta 28, km 7.5
1629 Pilar
Provincia de Buenos Aires
Argentina
PHONE: +54 11 4992-3724
EMAIL: alisgogo@gmail.com

PEPINO COSMICO
Carlos Alberto Pepe Laguardia /
Gonzalo Cordoba Zavalia
Panamericana Ramal, Pilar KM 40
1629 Pilar
Provincia de Buenos Aires
Argentina
PHONE: +54 911 5052-0127
EMAIL: c.laguardia@yahoo.com.ar

STUDIO GATTI
c/Puigcerdá,14
28001 Madrid
Spain
PHONE: +34 91 57 51 802
EMAIL: studiogatti@studiogatti.org

TRAMANDO
Martín Churba
Rodriguez Peña 1973
1021 Buenos Aires
Argentina
PHONE: +54 11 4811-0465
www.tramando.com

NADINE ZLOTOGORA
El Salvador 4638
1414 Buenos Aires
Argentina
PHONE: +54 11 4831-4203
www.nadinezlotogora.com

MERCADILLOS (FLEA MARKETS)

FERIA DE SAN PEDRO TELMO
Plaza Dorrego
Corner of Defensa and Humberto 1°
1430 Bueno Aires
Argentina
EMAIL: info@feriadesantelmo.com
www.feriadesantelmo.com

MERCADO DE LAS PULGAS DE DORREGO
Located in the block between Dorrego Avenida,
Conde, Gral. Enrique Martínez and Concepción Arenal
1414 Bueno Aires
Argentina

Acknowledgments / Danksagungen / Remerciements

I should like to give special thanks to Marie France Boyer for helping me to see Xul Solar's house from her own unique perspective, to Marie Paule Pellé for the idea of the photo of Oscar Galvez with Juan Manuel Fangio, and to Hugo Curletto for his valuable suggestions of addresses, without which this book would not have been the same.

Ricardo Labougle

Mein besonderer Dank gilt Marie France Boyer, die mir mit ihrem speziellen Blick geholfen hat, das Haus von Xul Solar zu entdecken, sowie Marie Paule Pellé für die Idee zum Foto von Oscar Galvez mit Juan Manuel Fangio. Hugo Curletto danke ich herzlich dafür, dass ich durch ihn einige Wohnhäuser kennenlernen durfte, ohne die dieses Buch nicht wäre, was es ist.

Ricardo Labougle

Je souhaite remercier tout particulièrement Marie France Boyer pour m'avoir fait découvrir, avec son regard si particulier, la maison de Xul Solar, Marie Paule Pellé pour l'idée de la photo de Oscar Galvez et de Juan Manuel Fangio ainsi qu'Hugo Curletto, pour m'avoir fait connaître quelques demeures sans lesquelles ce livre ne serait pas ce qu'il est.

Ricardo Labougle

ENDPAPERS / VORSATZPAPIER / PAGES DE GARDE
Dos Argentinos Oscar Galvez y Juan Manuel Fangio

PAGE 2 / SEITE 2 / PAGE 2
Kitchen table at Alan Faena's home, Buenos Aires / Küchentisch bei Alan Faena, Buenos Aires / Table de cuisine chez Alan Faena, Buenos Aires

PAGE 6 / SEITE 6 / PAGE 6
Confitería Ideal in the Centro district, Buenos Aires

To stay informed about upcoming TASCHEN titles, please request our magazine at www.taschen.com/magazine or write to TASCHEN, Hohenzollernring 53, D-50672 Cologne, Germany; contact@taschen.com; Fax: +49-221-254919. We will be happy to send you a free copy of our magazine, which is filled with information about all of our books.

© 2008 TASCHEN GmbH
Hohenzollernring 53, D–50672 Köln
www.taschen.com

Concept, editing and layout by
Angelika Taschen, Berlin
General project management by
Stephanie Bischoff, Cologne
Design by dieSachbearbeiter.*innen*, Berlin
English translation by Alayne Pullen for First Edition Translations Ltd, Cambridge
French translation by Philippe Safavi, Paris
German translation by Ingrid Hacker-Klier, Hebertsfelden
Lithography by Thomas Grell, Cologne

Printed in Germany

ISBN 978-3-8365-0845-2
(Edition with English / German cover)
ISBN 978-3-8365-0846-9
(Edition with French cover)

TASCHEN'S LIFESTYLE SERIES
EDITED BY ANGELIKA TASCHEN

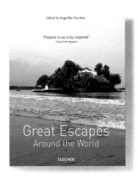

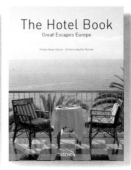

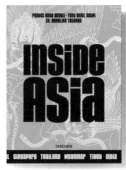
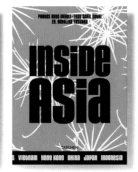

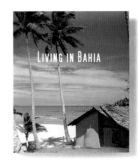

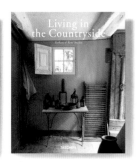

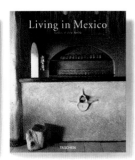
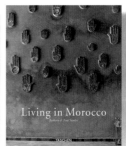

IN PREPARATION
NEW NEW YORK INTERIORS
ITALIAN INTERIORS
GREAT ESCAPES EUROPE, VOL. II
GREAT ESCAPES MEDITERRANEAN
TASCHEN'S PARIS
TASCHEN'S LONDON
TASCHEN'S BERLIN
TASCHEN'S NEW YORK